FAST & EASY
ENGLISH LEARNING

High Five 1

for your confidence and motivation

General English Conversation for Beginners

Author	Jooyoung Yoon
Chief Editor	Jiyou Min
Publisher	HiEnglish
First published	September 2018
Telephone	82-2-335-1002
Fax	82-2-6499-0219
Address	8 5 Angil Hongikro, Mapoku, Seoul, Korea
Homepage	www.hienglish.com
e-Mail	broadcast1@hienglish.com
Registered No.	2005-000040
ISBN	979-11-85342-38-2
	979-11-85342-37-5 (set)
Copyright	ⓒ 2018 HiEnglish
Price	KRW 18,000

No Unauthorized photocopying
All rights reserved. No part of this publication may be reproduced, stored in a retrieval system, or transmitted in any form or by any means, electronic, mechanical, photocopying, recording, or otherwise, without the prior permission of the publisher.

Preface

To our students;

This book was written specifically for Koreans who are begining to learn English. It contains Brainstorming, Grammar, Vocabulary, Dialogue, Practice, Application, and Discussion that would interest Korean learners.

High Five is carefully designed to meet the specific demands of Korean adults who need to speak better English for their careers and business. I hope this book will help Korean adult students start studying English in easy and interesting steps by growing their confidence.

The lessons in this book are up-to-date, realistic, and practical. It is my hope that students find this book entertaining, practical and helpful in their quest to become more fluent in the English language.

It is the mission of HiEnglish to support Korean's great global journey.

Jooyoung Yoon, c.e.o of HiEnglish

Contents
High Five

UNIT 01	**She is an American actress.** *Unit Goals* Be able to talk about jobs	9
UNIT 02	**He's an easygoing guy.** *Unit Goals* Be able to talk about personalities	17
UNIT 03	**There is a bag on the bench.** *Unit Goals* Be able to talk about where things are placed	25
UNIT 04	**You were very excited about the trip!** *Unit Goals* Be able to talk about emotions	33
UNIT 05	**I am tired of them.** *Unit Goals* Be able to talk about how you feel about something	41
UNIT 06	**It is hard to wake up early in the morning.** *Unit Goals* Be able to talk about what doing something is like	49
UNIT 07	**I got worried about you.** *Unit Goals* Be able to talk about what happened to you	57
UNIT 08	**It smells great!** *Unit Goals* Be able to talk about the five senses	65
UNIT 09	**It has been 7 years since I saw you.** *Unit Goals* Be able to talk about how long it has been since you did something	73
UNIT 10	**He talks too much.** *Unit Goals* Be able to talk about how something is done	81

High Five
Fast & Easy English Learning

UNIT 11	I couldn't sleep last night.	89
	Unit Goals Be able to talk about situations	

UNIT 12	I didn't attend the meeting.	97
	Unit Goals Be able to talk about meetings	

UNIT 13	I ask him for an autograph.	105
	Unit Goals Be able to talk about what you ask for	

UNIT 14	Did you send me a text?	113
	Unit Goals Be able to talkabout what you did	

UNIT 15	I stopped drinking.	121
	Unit Goals Be able to talk about what you stopped doing	

UNIT 16	You decided to learn English!	129
	Unit Goals Be able to talk about what you decided to do	

UNIT 17	I want you to give a presentation.	137
	Unit Goals Be able to talk about what you want someone to do	

UNIT 18	It made me cough.	145
	Unit Goals Be able to talk about what someone makes you do	

UNIT 19	Every time I try to play tennis, it rains.	153
	Unit Goals Be able to combine two sentences	

UNIT 20	I heard it's Edward.	161
	Unit Goals Be able to talk about what you heard and thought	

Appendix	Answer Key	169

Syllabus

Unit	Title	Learning Goal	Grammar	Vocabulary	Dialogue
01	She is an American actress.	Be able to talk about jobs	subject + be verb + noun	· housewife · actor · lawyer · celebrity	Actress
02	He's an easygoing guy.	Be able to talk about personalities	subject + be verb + adjective + noun	· easygoing · well-known · brave · friendly	New boss
03	There is a bag on the bench.	Be able to talk about where things are placed	there + be verb + subject + adverb phrase	· in · on · under · in front of	Bag on the bench
04	You were very excited about the trip!	Be able to talk about emotions	subject + be verb + emotive adjective	· embarrassed · confused · jealous · confident	Trip to Paris
05	I am tired of them.	Be able to talk about how you feel about something	subject + be verb + adjective + preposition + noun	· be happy with · be surprised at · be sure of · be worried about	Diet
06	It is hard to wake up early in the morning.	Be able to talk about what doing something is like	it + is + adjective + to + verb	· easy to take a taxi · better to speak in person · great to see you again	Daily life
07	I got worried about you.	Be able to talk about what happened to you	subject + got + adjective	· mad · hurt · worried · thirsty	Feelings
08	It smells great!	Be able to talk about the five senses	subject + sense verb + adjective	· taste, sound, smell, look, feel · sour · comfortable · sorry · ridiculous	Drinks
09	It has been 7 years since I saw you.	Be able to talk about how long it has been since you did something	It + has + been + ... + since + I + past verb + (noun)	· lengthy · endless · brief · temporary	Bumping into an old friend
10	He talks too much.	Be able to talk about how something is done	subject + verb + adverb	· talk · smile · stretch · cry · dance	New team members

Visit our website at www.pocketcampus.co.kr.
After signing up, you can access to the audio files.

Fast & Easy English Learning

Unit	Title	Learning Goal	Grammar	Vocabulary	Dialogue
11	I couldn't sleep last night.	Be able to talk about situations	subject + verb + adverb phrase	· last · exist · live · come · depart	Sleeping
12	I didn't attend the meeting.	Be able to talk about meetings	subject + verb + noun	· resemble · meet · lack · discuss	To miss a meeting
13	I ask him for an autograph.	Be able to talk about what you ask for	subject + verb + noun + for + noun	· ask · pay · thank	Concert
14	Did you send me a text?	Be able to talk about what you did	subject + verb + noun + noun	· lend · give · make · read	Giving a meeting schedule
15	I stopped drinking.	Be able to talk about what you stopped doing	subject + verb + verb-ing	· quit · consider · imagine · mind	After work plans
16	You decided to learn English!	Be able to talk about what you decided to do	subject + verb + to-verb	· tend · refuse · afford · wish	Studying English
17	I want you to give a presentation.	Be able to talk about what you want someone to do	subject + verb + noun + to-verb	· clean up · meet at the airport · send an email · Google it	Meeting reports
18	It made me cough.	Be able to talk about what someone makes you do	subject + causative verb + noun + verb or adjective	· make · let · have	Job interviews
19	Every time I try to play tennis, it rains.	Be able to combine two sentences	conjunction + subject + verb, subject + verb	· when · every time · as long as	Exercise
20	I heard it's Edward.	Be able to talk about what you heard and thought	subject + verb + (that) + subject + verb	· break up · work for Google · open a new restaurant · be my best friend	Promotions

High Five 1

for your confidence and motivation

UNIT 01

She is an American actress.

Unit Goals

Be able to talk about jobs.
Learn to use **"subject + be verb + noun"**

01 Brainstorming

Exercise 1 Read the story and underline the pattern where you see it in the box.

> Hello, everyone. **My name is** Paul Anton. I am forty-seven years old.
> I was a journalist for thirteen years, but I am currently a movie director.
> I worked with many actors and actresses in my movies.
> Most of them were Americans, but some of the actresses were Koreans. I like them, and they are still my friends.

Exercise 2 Fill in the blanks based on Paul's story. Then practice with your partner.

A What is his name?   **His name** _____ _____ .

B How old is he?   _____ _____ 47 years old.

C What is his job?   _____ _____ a movie director.

D What was his job?   **He was a** _____ .

E Where were most of the actors and actresses from?
Most of them _____ **Americans**.

10 HighFive 1

Grammar Focus

Subject	Be verb				Noun
	Present (positive)	Present (negative)	Past (positive)	Past (negative)	
I	am	am not	was	was not (wasn't)	a singer
You	are	are not (aren't)	were	were not (weren't)	a singer
We					singers
They					singers
He	is	is not (isn't)	was	was not (wasn't)	a singer
She					

Exercise 3 Read the conversation and fill in the blanks.

John: Hi. My name is John. Are you Esther?

Clara: No, I am not Esther. My name is Clara.

John: Oh, I am sorry. I am a new member of the sales team.

Clara: It's nice to meet you, John.

John: Nice to meet you, too.

Clara: Esther is our team leader. She is in the meeting room. She is the only Asian woman in there.

John: Oh, I see. Thank you.

Positive	Negative
John _____ a new team member.	John _____ a team leader.
Esther _____ a team leader.	Clara _____ a new team member.
_____ an Asian woman.	Esther and Clara _____ friends.

Unit1 She is an American actress 11

03 Vocabulary

Exercise 4 Match the words in the box with pictures a–f

housewife   actor   lawyer   celebrity   office worker   journalist

a   b   c   d   e   f

Exercise 5 Fill in the blanks with the appropriate words.

A I am a very famous singer in America
I am an American _____.

B My friend is a married woman and looks after her home and children.
She _____.

C My brother acted in films ten years ago, but he writes news articles now.
_____ an actor, but he _____ now.

D My wife works for a company and gets paid monthly.
_____.

E My parents advise people about the law and represent them in court.
They _____.

04 Dialogue

Exercise 6 Look at the conversation. Fill in the blanks with the appropriate words from the box below. Then listen to the conversation and practice with your partner.

> She   is she   actress   is her   she is   she is not   old is she   That's

Gina: Oh my! Look at her. _____ Anne Hathaway!

Sam: Who _____?

Gina: _She is_ an American _actress_.

Sam: What _____ name again?

Gina: Anne Hathaway. She played a main character in "The Devil Wears Prada."

Sam: I watched the movie, but I don't remember her. I thought _____ Amanda Seyfried.

Gina: No, _____ Amanda Seyfried.

Sam: I see. How _____?

Gina: _____ 36 years old.

Sam: Oh, she looks very young. Let's take a photo with her.

Gina: _____ a good idea!

Unit1 She is an American actress   13

05 Practice

Exercise 7 Ask and answer the questions about the people in the pictures.

e.g.
- Q: What's his name? — A: His name is Jake Smith.
- Q: How old is he? — A: He is forty years old.
- Q: What is his job? — A: He is a lawyer.

A
- Jessica Miller — Q: _____ A: _____
- 22 years old — Q: _____ A: _____
- Cheerleader — Q: _____ A: _____

B
- Andrew Horton — Q: _____ A: _____
- 53 years old — Q: _____ A: _____
- Priest — Q: _____ A: _____

C
- Chloe Rodgers — Q: _____ A: _____
- 31 years old — Q: _____ A: _____
- Fashion designer — Q: _____ A: _____

Exercise 8 Pair work – Ask and answer the questions about Harry.

Harry Linden
Chief manager

Hi RESTAURANT

- 380-450-3915 (office)
- 614-948-2531 (mobile)
- linden.harry@oia.org

14 HighFive 1

06 Application

Exercise 9 Use the words below and describe who you are.

> homemaker   actor   lawyer   celebrity
> office worker   journalist

name

age

job

07 Discussion

Exercise 10 Read the following story and fill in the blanks with the given words. Share your ideas with your partner and present them to the whole class.

① popularity ② host ③ competitions ④ released ⑤ tournament

Korea's E-Sports Enters New Market

Korea's e-sports are beginning to hold __A__ with smartphone games because of their __B__ in Korea. Before, e-sports games in Korea used online games made in other countries. Now, e-sports are starting to use Korean games for their competitions. Companies such as XYZ and ABC Games have been pushing to make their smartphone games part of Korea's e-sports competitions for three years. They are already starting to see great results when XYZ __C__ "Wizard's War" it became the one of the most successful smartphone games in Korea. From there, XYZ started a gaming competition using "Wizard's War" that was held in cities all over the world such as Los Angeles, New York, Paris, Tokyo, and Seoul. Also, ABC Games made a popular game that they wish to use in competitions. The company plans to __D__ a gaming __E__ in Seoul. Twelve teams from countries like Taiwan, Vietnam, Indonesia, and Korea will compete for the championship. Six hundred million won in prize money will be given to the winners, which is the largest amount so far awarded in an e-sports competition. Now, ABC Games hopes that the competitions will get many people to watch the games and, hopefully, make the tournament more popular.

Q1 What do you think about the spread of the playing e-sports? Do you think it is good for our society?

Q2 Are you interesting in e-sports? Do you know anyone who is a fan of online games?

16 HighFive 1

02 UNIT

He's an easygoing guy.

Unit Goals

Be able to talk about personalities.
Learn to use **"subject + be verb + adjective + noun"**

01 Brainstorming

Exercise 1 **What do you think about yourself?**
Read the statements and put checks (v) in the boxes.

I am…	Yes	No	Not sure
I am a kind person.			
I am a good listener.			
I am a humorous person.			

Exercise 2 Ask and answer the questions based on your answers from above. Then practice with your partner.

A
Are you a kind person?
Yes / No, _____ a kind person.

B
Are you a _____ ?
Yes / No, _____ a good listener.

C
Are you a humorous person?
Yes / No, _____ .

18 HighFive 1

Grammar Focus

Adjective	Examples
A word that describes a person or thing.	**big** house **nice** guy **beautiful** flower
A word that usually comes before a noun or after the be-verb.	I am **fast**. He is a **smart** boy. It is **cheap**. She is a **new** customer.

Exercise 3 Read the following story and answer the following questions.

Hi Jules. Let me tell you about my favorite musician. His name is Bruno Mars. He is a famous American singer. He was born on a beautiful island, Oahu, in Hawaii. His parents were also popular musicians. He was a big fan of Elvis Presley and Michael Jackson when he was a young boy.

A. Find the adjectives in Jules' story. Then fill in the table and share the answers with your partner.

Adjective	Examples
favorite	He is a famous American singer.

B. Ask and answer the questions about Jules' story. Then practice with your partner.

A
Who is Jules' favorite musician?
Her _____ is Bruno Mars.

B
Is he a _____ British singer?
No, _____ a famous British singer.

03 Vocabulary

Exercise 4 Match the words on the left with the meanings on the right.

easygoing	a	1	kind to other people
well-known	b	2	excellent
brave	c	3	only like a small range of things
friendly	d	4	relaxed
amazing	e	5	have clear rules
picky	f	6	do not show fear
lucky	g	7	support people
strict	h	8	famous
helpful	i	9	shy and quiet
introverted	j	10	good things happen to the person

Exercise 5 Make three sentences using some of the words above. Then share them with your partner. (Subject + be verb + adjective + noun)

e.g. He is a strict guy.

A My friend is _____.

B _____.

C _____.

04 Dialogue

Exercise 6 — Look at the conversation. Fill in the blanks with the appropriate words from the box below. Then listen to the conversation and practice with your partner.

| He is | well-known | introverted | brave | Is he | helpful | easygoing |

Jane: Hey look! _____ the new head of our department. His name is Harrison Rods.

Gabe: _____ a nice person? He looks very strict.

Jane: He's an ___easygoing___ guy. He is also very friendly.

Gabe: How do you know about him?

Jane: He's a _____ financial specialist.

Gabe: Really? I didn't know that.

Jane: He's also very _____. He will help you at anytime.

Gabe: That's good.

Jane: Let's go to talk to him. Come on!

Gabe: Well... I'm a quite _____ person. It's hard for me to talk to strangers.

Jane: Be _____! You can do it.

Unit2 He's an easygoing guy

05 Practice

Exercise 7 Introduce the people in the box to your partner.

e.g.

Her name is Laura Olsen.
She is twenty-six years old.
She talks to strangers easily.
She is sociable.

A

Brad Carter   37 years old   drinks beer   heavy drinker

B

Ellen Baker   4 years old   doesn't like vegetables   picky eater

C

Jenny Cox   9 years old   learns new things fast   fast learner

Exercise 8 Story telling – Look at the picture of Dana Spencer and make a story about her. Then share it with your partner.

Her name is Dana Spencer.

06 Application

Exercise 9 Use the words below and describe what kind of person your partner is.

> easygoing   well-known   brave   friendly   amazing
> picky   lucky   strict   helpful   introverted

age

character

job

hobby

07 Discussion

Exercise 10 Read the following story and fill in the blanks with the given words. Share your ideas with your partner and present them to the whole class.

① similar   ② politician   ③ affect   ④ passed   ⑤ substances

Korean government supports increase in e-cigarette tax

The Korean government is debating an increase in taxes on e-cigarettes. They say they want to increase the price from 4,300 won to 5,000 won. If the bill __A__, the higher tax will begin in the middle of December.

Before, e-cigarettes were in a different tax group from regular cigarettes. That's why e-cigarettes were taxed at a lower rate. Many companies, like Johnson Tobacco and TAC Cigarettes sold e-cigarettes because of the lower tax. Now, these companies say that the new tax will make the price of e-cigarettes more expensive. They say that the price could raise to over 5,000 won.

Cigarette company officials say that the tax can __B__ the cost of making e-cigarettes. Some companies are already saying that they might have to increase their prices, which will affect their customers. However, a government ministry says that prices might not go higher. They say that e-cigarettes in Japan have a high tax, but their prices are __C__ to regular cigarettes. A __D__ from Korea's conservative political party plans to present the bill to raise the tax on e-cigarette because of the harmful __E__ e-cigarettes have.

Q1 Do you agree that the taxes on e-cigarettes should increase?

Q2 Do you think it is appropriate for the Korean government to compare of Japan's high tax on e-cigarette to Korea's situation?

03 UNIT

There is a bag on the bench.

Unit Goals

Be able to talk about where things are placed.
Learn to use **"there + be verb + subject + adverb phrase"**

01 Brainstorming

Exercise 1 What's on the desk? Write what you see in the cloud.

a laptop

two pencils

Exercise 2 Complete the sentences based on the picture above.

A _____ _____ a pen.

B _____ _____ an eraser.

C There are two _____ .

D _____ _____ a cell phone.

E _____ _____ a cup.

F There _____ two pencils.

G _____ _____ a laptop.

H _____ _____ a cell phone.

On the desk, there is one pen, one _____ , one _____ ,
and one _____ .
And, there are two _____ , two _____ ,
and three electronic devices (e.g. mobile, laptop).

26 HighFive 1

02 Grammar

Grammar Focus

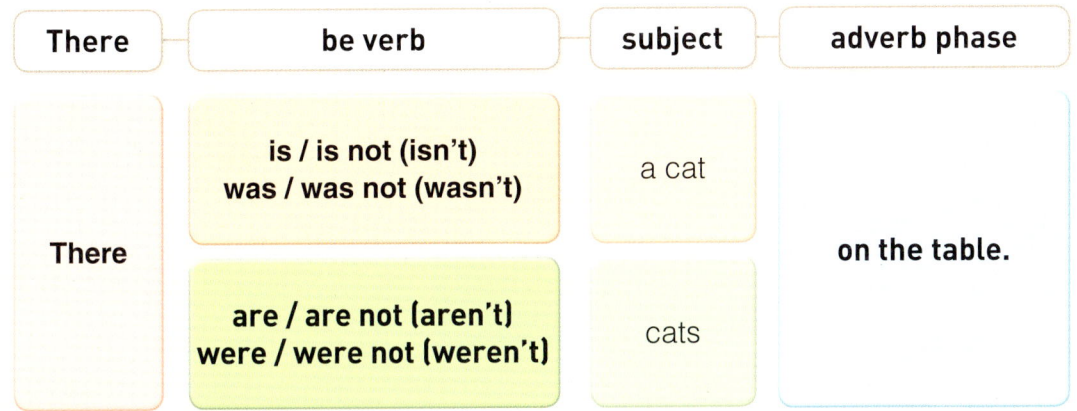

Exercise 3 Look at the pictures and complete the sentences in the box. Then share the answers with your partner.

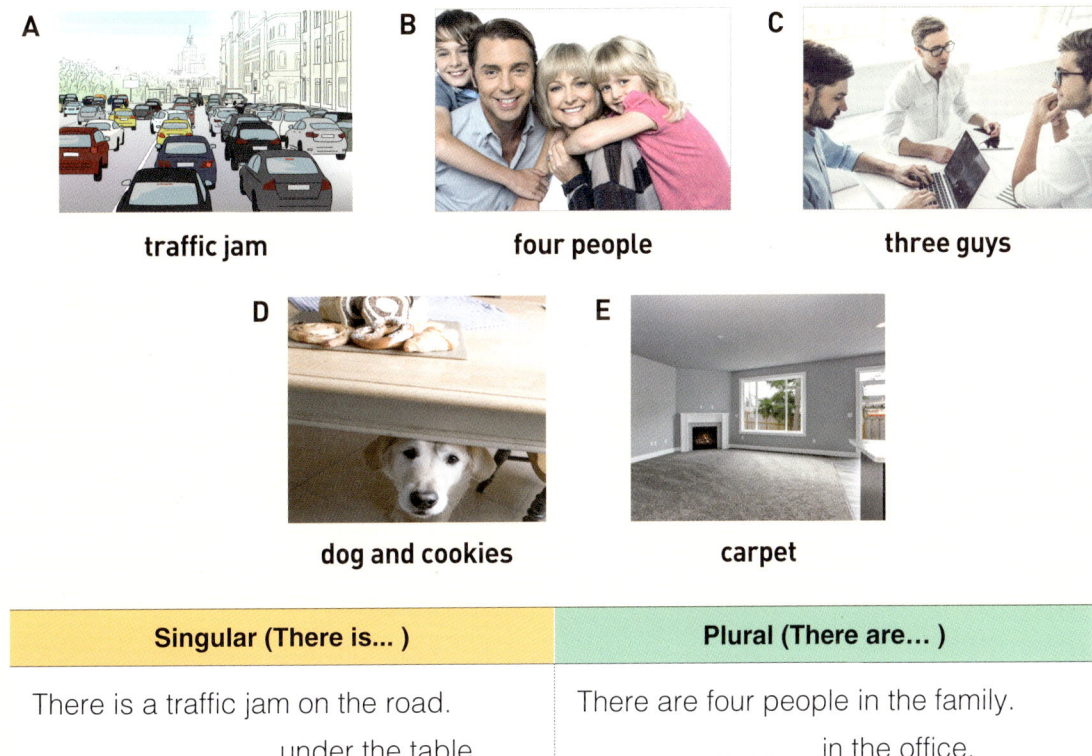

A traffic jam
B four people
C three guys
D dog and cookies
E carpet

Singular (There is…)	Plural (There are…)
There is a traffic jam on the road.	There are four people in the family.
_____ under the table.	_____ in the office.
_____ on the floor.	_____ on the table.

Unit3 There is a bag on the bench

03 Vocabulary

Exercise 4 Complete the sentences based on the pictures, and practice with your partner.

A B C

D E F

e.g. Is there a girl in the box?
▶ Yes, *there is a girl in the box*.

A _____ three girls _____ the tree?
▶ Yes, there _____.

B Is there a guy _____?
▶ Yes, there is _____.

C _____ a boy _____ the door?
▶ Yes, there _____ the door.

D Is there a guy _____ the sofa?
▶ Yes, there is _____.

E Is _____ the cat?
▶ Yes, there is a dog _____ the cat.

04 Dialogue

Exercise 6 Look at the conversation. Fill in the blanks with the appropriate words from the box below. Then listen to the conversation and practice with your partner.

```
in   isn't   there was   on   There is   there a cell phone in the bag   Is there   was there
```

Suzy: Excuse me, sir. _There was_ a bag on the bench over there.

Police officer: Oh, _____ anyone sitting next to the bag?

Suzy: No, there was no one nearby.

Police officer: I see. Let me check the bag. (Searching the bag)

Suzy: _____ a wallet _____ the bag?

Police officer: Yes, there is. But, there isn't an ID card _____ the wallet.

Suzy: Hmm… What about a cell phone? Is _____ _____?

Police officer: No, there _____. Was there anything next to the bag?

Suzy: Oh, _____ a business card _____ the bench. Here it is.

Police officer: Good! _____ a phone number on the card. Maybe we can find the owner. Thank you!

05 Practice

Exercise 6 Look at the picture of Matt's living room. Fill in the blanks, then practice with your partner.

e.g.
- Q <u>Is there</u> a sofa in the living room?
- A Yes, there is. <u>There is</u> a green sofa.

A
- Q Is there a cat under the sofa?
- A No, there isn't. _____ a cat on the sofa.

B
- Q _____ cushions on the sofa?
- A Yes, there are. There are three cushions on the sofa.

C
- Q _____ there books on the bookshelf?
- A Yes, _____ some books on the bookshelf.

D
- Q _____ a cup on the floor?
- A No, _____ . There _____ on the table.

E
- Q _____ flowerpots on the bookshelf?
- A Yes, _____ two flowerpots on the top of the bookshelf.

30 HighFive 1

 **Application**

Exercise 7   What's in your room? Draw a picture of your room in the box and describe it to your partner.

This is my room. There is a bed in my room.

07 Discussion

Exercise 8 Read the following story and fill in the blanks with the given words. Share your ideas with your partner and present them to the whole class.

① symptoms   ② rodents   ③ affects   ④ organs   ⑤ cloned

Scientists make pig with Alzheimer's

Scientists from Jeju National University made the first ever __A__ pig that has three __B__ of Alzheimer's. The cloned pig, called "JNUPIG," will be used in medical research for dementia and other mental diseases. Alzheimer's is a problem that __C__ humans, and scientists believe the research from cloned pigs like JNUPIG can help in developing medicine to fight against Alzheimer's.

A professor that helped to make JNUPIG believes the research could help economically, too. The technology created to study Alzheimer's in pigs can generate much money for companies that want to make medicine for Alzheimer's. Alzheimer's is a disease that destroys brain cells. Researchers used __D__ to study Alzheimer's. However, the results were not helpful because a rodent's __E__ are different from a human's. Pigs were seen as a better choice because their organ parts and structure are similar to human's.

In 2009, scientists in Denmark created a pig that had dementia. However, that pig only had one factor that causes Alzheimer's, not the three that are needed to create Alzheimer's. The first JNUPIG created died showing symptoms that were very similar to those shown by humans.

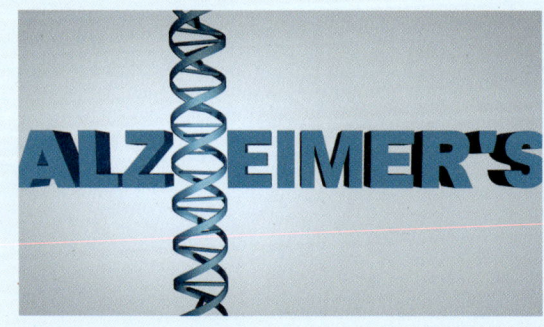

Q1 Do you agree that animals should be used for medical research? What are the pros and cons of animal testing?

Q2 Why is dementia considered a critical social problem?

UNIT 04

You were very excited about the trip!

Unit Goals

Be able to talk about emotions.
Learn to use **"subject + be verb + emotive adjective"**

01 Brainstorming

Exercise 1 Match the emotions on the left with the pictures on the right. Write the appropriate emotions under the pictures.

Emotions

- curious
- angry
- happy
- sorry
- nervous
- sleepy

Happy

Exercise 2 Fill in the blanks with the words above.

A My friend has lots of secrets. I am _____ about her secrets.

B I broke my friend's cell phone. I was so _____ .

C I am _____ now because I have a job interview tomorrow.

D My husband lied to me. I was very _____ .

E My boyfriend proposed to me yesterday. I was so _____ .

02 Grammar

Grammar Focus
Different forms of emotive adjectives – verbs become adjectives!

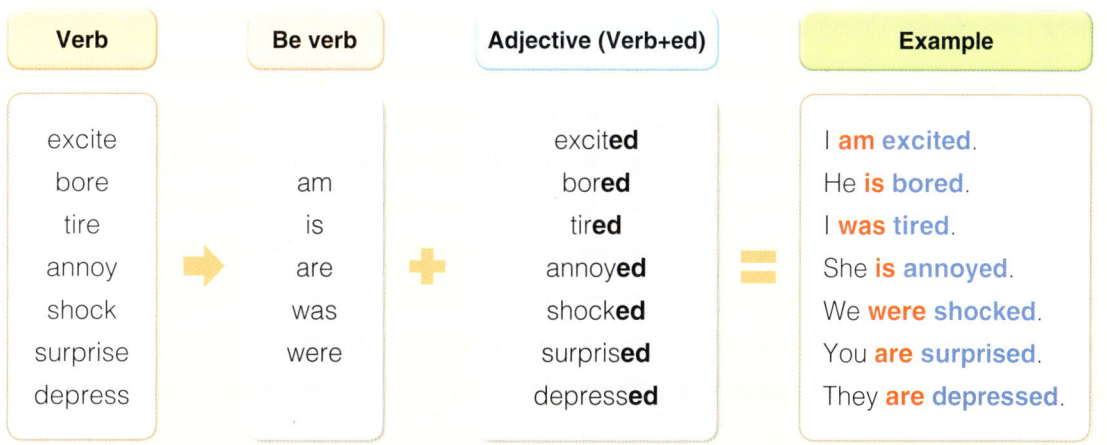

Verb	Be verb	Adjective (Verb+ed)	Example
excite	am	excit**ed**	I **am** excited.
bore	is	bor**ed**	He **is** bored.
tire	are	tir**ed**	I **was** tired.
annoy	was	annoy**ed**	She **is** annoyed.
shock	were	shock**ed**	We **were** shocked.
surprise		surpris**ed**	You **are** surprised.
depress		depress**ed**	They **are** depressed.

Exercise 3 Look at the pictures and the conversation. Then fill in the blanks with appropriate emotive adjectives.

- **A** How was the movie?
- **B** It was good, but I _was annoyed_ because a guy was talking on the phone.

- **A** Are you OK?
- **B** I am _____. I got F for Math.

- **A** Hi John. How are you today?
- **B** I ____ _____. I worked overtime yesterday.

03 Vocabulary

Exercise 4 Look at the pictures and the words. Then read the sentences about the six people and fill in the blanks with the appropriate words.

jealous   confused   embarrassed

confident   disappointed   calm

| e.g. | Amy | Jane bought a new nice dress. I'm very ___jealous___. |

| A | Helen | In a team meeting, we had an argument, but Jake was so _____. |

| B | Eugene | I got a birthday gift from my boyfriend yesterday, but I didn't like it. I was _____. |

| C | Jake | What day is it today? Is it Sunday or Monday? I'm very _____. |

| D | Tom | I am very good at driving. I'm quite _____. |

| F | Sally | I went to a supermarket yesterday, but I didn't have any money. I was so _____. |

04 Dialogue

Exercise 6 Look at the conversation. Fill in the blanks with the appropriate words from the box below. Then listen to the conversation and practice with your partner.

embarrassed   excited   happy   depressed   annoyed

Luke: Victoria! How was your trip to Paris?

Victoria: Well, it wasn't good.

Luke: What happened? You were very _excited_ about the trip.

Victoria: I lost my bag in the airport. I was so _____.

Luke: Oh no!

Victoria: But an airport worker found my bag, so I was really _____.

Luke: That was lucky!

Victoria: But, the flight was delayed for five hours.

Luke: Oh my! How did you feel?

Victoria: I _____ very _____.

Luke: Did you have a good time in Paris?

Victoria: Well, I lost my phone on the first day of my trip...

Unit4 You were very excited about the trip!

05 Practice

Exercise 6 Look at the pictures about Carrie's day. Then guess how she felt in each situation and complete the sentences. (Answers may vary)

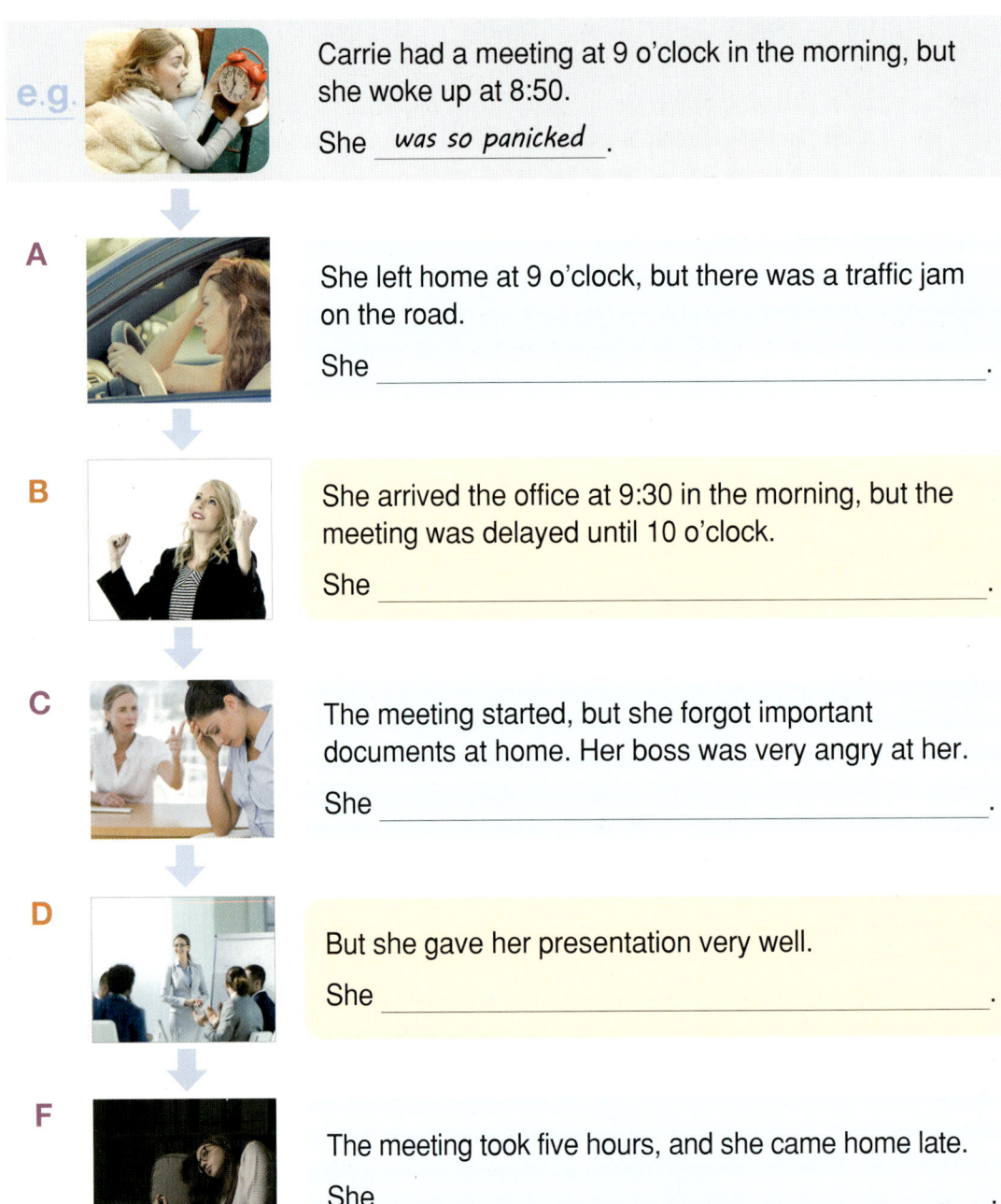

e.g. Carrie had a meeting at 9 o'clock in the morning, but she woke up at 8:50.
She _was so panicked_.

A She left home at 9 o'clock, but there was a traffic jam on the road.
She _____.

B She arrived the office at 9:30 in the morning, but the meeting was delayed until 10 o'clock.
She _____.

C The meeting started, but she forgot important documents at home. Her boss was very angry at her.
She _____.

D But she gave her presentation very well.
She _____.

F The meeting took five hours, and she came home late.
She _____.

06 Application

Exercise 7 Ask and answer the questions with your partner by using the expressions below.

e.g. *How do you feel about.......*

Q How do you feel about eating spicy food?
A I'm scared.

A
Q _____ going abroad?
A _____.

B
Q _____ having a meeting with your client or boss?
A _____.

C
Q _____ going shopping?
A _____.

D
Q _____ driving a car?
A _____.

E
Q _____ attending a company dinner?
A _____.

Unit4 You were very excited about the trip!

07 Discussion

Exercise 8 Read the following story and fill in the blanks with the given words. Share your ideas with your partner and present them to the whole class.

① advance   ② debut   ③ loss   ④ presented   ⑤ expose   ⑥ participate

Taekwondo will appear at the Paralympics in 2020

Taekwondo will make its __A__ at the 2020 Paralympics in Tokyo. Seventy-two athletes will compete in six medal competitions. The International Taekwondo Association __B__ its plan for the Paralympics in London, where the plan was approved. The medal competitions will be divided : three for men and three for women. Athletes that can __C__ in the event must have at least the __D__ of one hand up to the wrist. The competitions will be held over three days, with two medal events happening each day. Another competition talked about in London was the Global Taekwondo Championship. Global Taekwondo began championship games to __E__ the profile of top-ranked athletes and __F__ the sport to the world. The championship games have eight tournaments for each Olympic weight group. Four for men and four for women.

Today, Taekwondo is becoming more popular. With events like the Paralympics, the future of Taekwondo as a sport appears to be bright. Taekwondo groups continue to promote the sport throughout the world to achieve greater recognition.

Q1 Do you think Koreans have an advantage in Taekwondo competitions because Taekwondo is a Korean national sport? If not, why?

Q2 What makes specific sports popular worldwide?

UNIT 05

I am tired of them.

Unit Goals

Be able to talk about how you feel about something.
Learn to use **"subject + be verb + adjective + preposition + noun"**

01 Brainstorming

Exercise 1 Look at the words in the speech bubble and divide them into the three boxes: crazy about, scared of, or tired of. (e.g. if you like horror movies, put the word in the "crazy about" box)

*horror movies
staying home alone
roller-coaster rides
traveling alone
spicy food*

Crazy about (Like a lot)	Scared of	Tired of (don't like anymore)

Exercise 2 Answer the questions using your answers above. Then practice with your partner.

A
Are you **scared of** watching horror movies?
Yes, *I'm scared of* watching horror movies.
No, *I'm not scared of* watching horror movies.

B
Are you **tired of** staying home alone?
Yes / No, _____ staying home alone.

C
Are you **crazy about** roller-coaster rides?
Yes / No, _____ roller-coaster rides.

D
Are you **scared of** traveling alone?
Yes / No, _____ traveling alone.

E
Are you **crazy about** spicy food?
Yes / No, _____ spicy food.

02 Grammar

Grammar focus

be verb	adjective	preposition	noun
am / am not are / aren't is / isn't was / wasn't were / weren't	tired scared	of of	driving
	crazy excited nervous	about about about	

Exercise 3 Look at the pictures and answer the questions based on the pictures. Then practice with your partner.

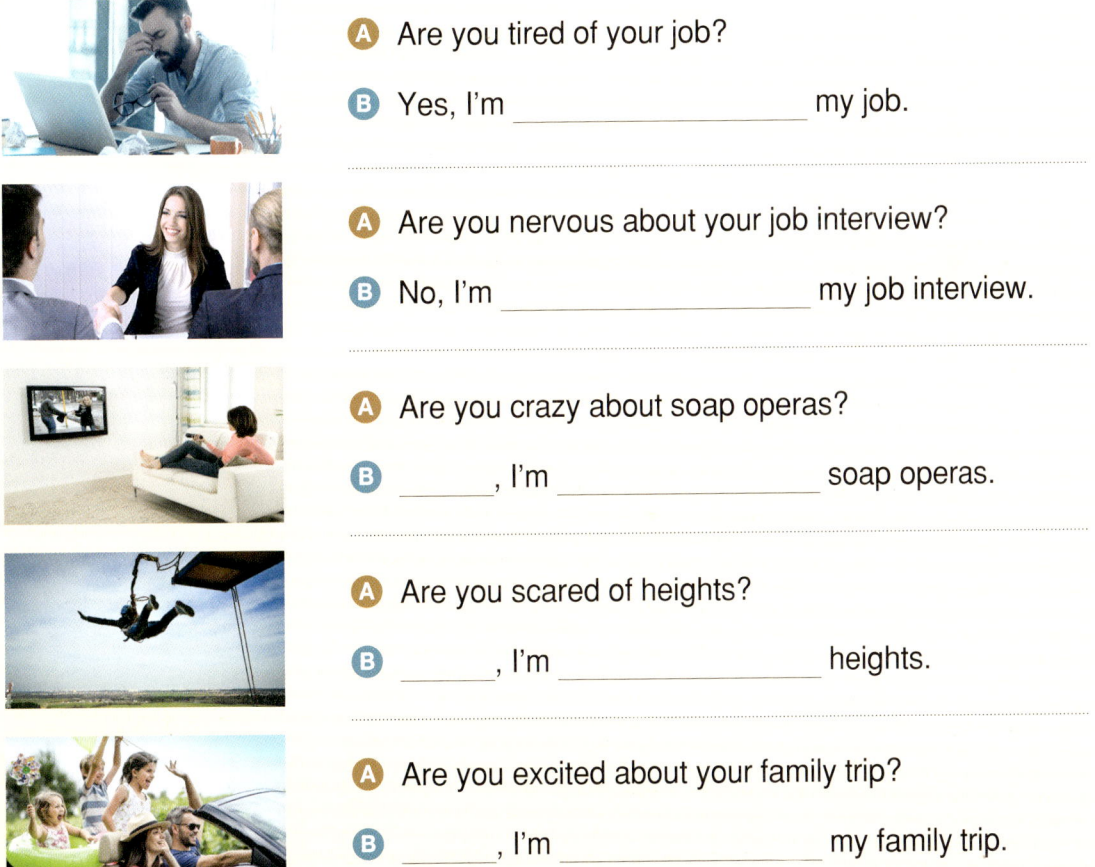

Ⓐ Are you tired of your job?

Ⓑ Yes, I'm _____ my job.

Ⓐ Are you nervous about your job interview?

Ⓑ No, I'm _____ my job interview.

Ⓐ Are you crazy about soap operas?

Ⓑ _____, I'm _____ soap operas.

Ⓐ Are you scared of heights?

Ⓑ _____, I'm _____ heights.

Ⓐ Are you excited about your family trip?

Ⓑ _____, I'm _____ my family trip.

Unit5 I am tired of them   43

03 Vocabulary

Exercise 4 Look at the conversations and complete the sentences with the appropriate "adjective+preposition". Then practice with your partner.

be happy with	be surprised at
be sure of	be worried about	be disappointed in

e.g.
- **Matthew**: Hey Mark, did you hear the news?
- **Mark**: Oh yes, I was _surprised at_ the news.

A
- **Billy**: Do you like your job as an English teacher?
- **Grace**: Yes! I am _____ my job.

B
- **Eva**: Congratulations! You passed the job interview.
- **Thomas**: Thank you. I _____ the result.

C
- **Brad**: I heard that your boyfriend lied to you.
- **Olivia**: Yes... I _____ him.

D
- **Emily**: Your son scratched my son's face!
- **Jessica**: He didn't do it. _____ it.

Exercise 5 Fill in the blanks to complete the questions based on the given answers.

e.g. _Is_ she _scared of_ dogs? ▶ No, she isn't scared of dogs.

A _____ you _____ your boss' behavior?
▶ Yes, I'm disappointed in my boss' behavior.

B _____ _____ _____ his size? ▶ No, I'm not sure of his size.

C _____ he _____ his presentation?
▶ Yes, he's worried about his presentation.

44 HighFive 1

04 Dialogue

Exercise 6 Look at the conversation. Fill in the blanks with the appropriate words from the box below. Then listen to the conversation and practice with your partner.

| jealous of | surprised at | scared of | tired of | worried about | disappointed in |

Jacob: Are you on a diet?

Carol: Yes, I eat only chicken breast salads.

Jacob: Do you like them?

Carol: No! I am _tired of_ them.

Jacob: Did you lose some weight?

Carol: Only 1kg. I am so _____ myself.

Jacob: You know what? Liz lost 5kg!

Carol: I know. I was very _____ the news. I am so _____ her.

Jacob: I am _____ your health. You need to eat balanced meals.

Carol: I know, but I'm _____ gaining weight.

Unit5 I am tired of them 45

05 Practice

Exercise 7 Look at the pictures and the tables. Then ask and answers questions about them with your partner.

Name	Abbey
Situation	She is going to college this year
How does the person feel?	Excited

e.g.
- Ⓐ Abbey is going to college this year.
- Ⓑ Is she excited about it?
- Ⓐ Yes, she is very excited!

A

Name	Chris
Situation	He plays computer games every day.
How does the person feel?	Happy

Ⓐ ....
Ⓑ ....
Ⓐ ....

B

Name	Helen and James
Situation	They are moving to a new city next week.
How do they feel?	Worried

Ⓐ ....
Ⓑ ....
Ⓐ ....

06 Application

Exercise 8 Ask and answer the questions with your partner using the expression below.

e.g. *Do you like …….*

Q <u>Do you like</u> meeting new people?
A No, <u>I'm very nervous about</u> meeting new people.

A
Q _____ listening to K-pop?
A _____.

B
Q _____ drinking alcohol?
A _____.

C
Q _____ exploring new places?
A _____.

D
Q _____ staying home on the weekend?
A _____.

E
Q _____ trying new foods?
A _____.

Unit5 I am tired of them

07 Discussion

Exercise 9 Read the following story and fill in the blanks with the given words. Share your ideas with your partner and present them to the whole class.

① insults   ② negotiating   ③ diplomats   ④ tensions
⑤ contradict   ⑥ explodes

Trump wants to solve North Korean problem peacefully

American President Donald Trump wants to follow a peaceful path unless a nuclear bomb __A__ over the United States. Secretary of State Rex Tillerson, in an interview with CNN, said that __B__ have increased because of North Korea's nuclear and missile programs. Secretary Tillerson says he wants to find a peaceful solution. However, President Trump seemed to __C__ Secretary Tillerson on the social media website, Twitter, by saying that Tillerson is "wasting his time __D__." Trump even called North Korean leader Kim Jong-un "Little Rocket Man." The President's tweet caused some __E__ to worry, but Secretary Tillerson has said that the President was trying to get people to get serious about negotiating peace.

Secretary Tillerson says that he and the President want the North Korean government to know that all options, including military options, are open for discussion. North Korea has performed a series of missile and nuclear tests recently, showing a greater ability to hit the US with a nuclear weapon. President Trump and Kim have been throwing __F__ at each and have threatened to use military force against each other.

Q1 What do you think is the best way to lessen international tensions, negotiations or using pressure?

Q2 Why do you think Western powers are involved in making a peace between other countries?

UNIT 06

It is hard to wake up early in the morning.

Unit Goals

Be able to talk about what doing something is like.
Learn to use **"it + is + adjective + to + verb"**

01 Brainstorming

Exercise 1 Look at the words in the box and divide them between the two circles: "easy to do" and "hard to do." (e.g. if cooking is easy, put "cook" in the "easy to do" box)

"Easy to do"

cook
talk to strangers
lose weight
say no
wake up early

"Hard to do"

Exercise 2 Answer the questions based on your responses above. Then practice with your partner.

A Is it easy to cook?
Yes, *it is easy to* cook. / No, *it is hard to* cook.

B Is it easy to talk to strangers?
Yes / No, _____ talk to strangers.

C Is it easy to lose weight?
Yes / No, _____ lose weight.

D Is it easy to say no?
Yes / No, _____ say no.

02 Grammar

Grammar Focus

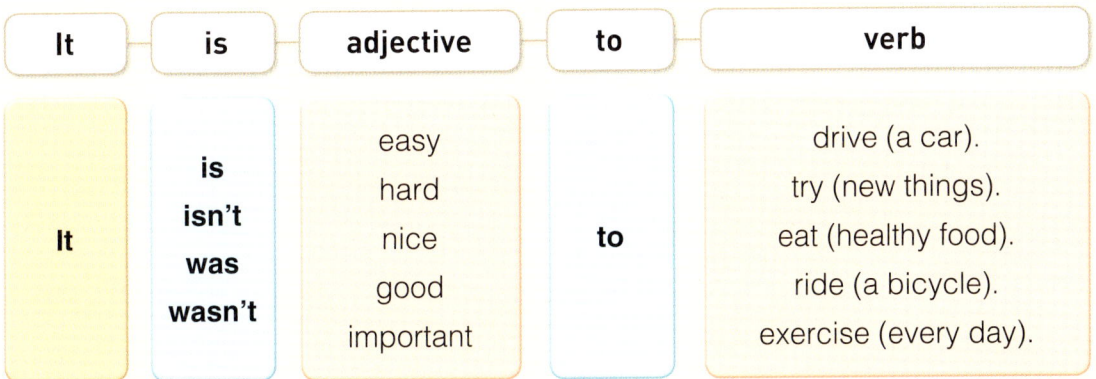

Exercise 3 Look at the questions and fill in the blanks based on your opinion. Then practice with your partner.

A
- Ⓐ Is it easy to drive a car?
- Ⓑ No, it _isn't easy to_ drive a car.

B
- Ⓐ Is it important to eat healthy food?
- Ⓑ Yes / No, it _____ eat healthy food.

C
- Ⓐ Is it nice to try new things?
- Ⓑ Yes / No, it _____ try new things.

D
- Ⓐ Is it difficult to ride a bicycle?
- Ⓑ Yes / No, it _____ ride a bicycle.

E
- Ⓐ Is it good to exercise every day?
- Ⓑ Yes / No, it _____ exercise every day.

03 Vocabulary

Exercise 4 There are two boxes below: adjectives and verb phrases. Make five sentences, each with one adjective and one verb phrase.

Adjectives
- easy
- difficult
- better
- great
- important

Verb phrases
- speak in person
- take a taxi
- see you again
- hear your voice
- remember people's names
- blame others

e.g. Q It's _easy_ to _blame others_.

A It isn't _____ to _____.
B It's _____ to _____.
C It isn't _____ to _____.
D It's _____ to _____.
E It's _____ to _____.

Exercise 5 Fill in the blanks to complete the questions based on the given answers.

e.g. Is it hard to work late? ▶ Yes, it is hard to work late.

A _____ it _____ finish the book?
▶ No, it's not difficult to finish the book.

B Was _____ to move the furniture?
▶ No, it wasn't easy to move the furniture.

C _____ to turn left here?
▶ Yes, it's better to turn left here.

04 Dialogue

Exercise 6 Look at the conversation. Fill in the blanks with the appropriate words from the box below. Then listen to the conversation and practice with your partner.

| difficult | interesting | important | better | easy |

Amy: Robert, did you wake up early today?

Robert: No, it _is hard to_ wake up early in the morning.

Amy: Well, it _____ go to bed early.

Robert: I know, but it isn't _____ stop watching TV at night.

Amy: What did you watch last night?

Robert: I watched "House of Cards."

Amy: Is it _____ watch?

Robert: Yes, it is. You should watch it.

Amy: What about "Dark"?

Robert: Hmm, it's a little bit _____ understand the story.

Amy: Anyway, you have a team meeting tomorrow morning. It _____ wake up early tomorrow!

Robert: OK, don't worry.

05 Practice

Exercise 7 Look at the pictures and key words. Then ask and answer questions about the pictures using the key words and appropriate adjectives. (Answers may vary)

e.g.

Key words lift dumbbells

Ⓐ _Is it hard to_ lift dumbbells?
Ⓑ _Yes, it is hard_ (to lift dumbbells).

A

Key words go to Europe in summer

Ⓐ
Ⓑ

B

Key words drive a car during rush hour

Ⓐ
Ⓑ

C

Key words watch horror movies at night

Ⓐ
Ⓑ

D

Key words eat breakfast in the morning

Ⓐ
Ⓑ

54 HighFive 1

06 Application

Exercise 8 Look at the questions and give your answers. Then practice with your partner.

e.g.
Q Is it easy to talk to new people?
A No, _it isn't easy to_ talk to new people.

A
Q Is it nice to go mountain climbing in winter?
A _____.

B
Q Is it important to attend a company dinner?
A _____.

C
Q Is it difficult to learn new languages?
A _____.

Unit6 It is hard to wake up early in the morning

07 Discussion

Exercise 9 Read the following story and fill in the blanks with the given words. Share your ideas with your partner and present them to the whole class.

① removal   ② replaced   ③ efforts   ④ purpose   ⑤ ministry

Government to remove foreign words from school textbooks

The Ministry of Education plans to slowly remove foreign words in elementary school textbooks. The __A_____ is to help young students better learn their native Korean language. The school textbooks will remove a total of 322 foreign words in the third and fourth grade textbooks. The words will be __B_____ with Korean words in the new textbook editions. Most of the words being replaced are Korean pronunciations of English, Chinese and Japanese words. For example, in one third grade textbook, the English word knife is used. Textbook researchers have offered to replace the word with the Korean word kal. Other words targeted for replacement are guest, greenbelt, balance, campfire, camping, handsome, and helmet.

As well, many Japanese-style expressions like maejang for store, jibulhada for pay and saryo for feed, will be replaced by Korean words. The __C_____ of these foreign words is being done to help advance the Korean language in the new textbooks. Eventually, __D_____ will be made to remove Chinese-style expressions from elementary school books. The __E_____ says it will focus on foreign words in fifth and sixth grade textbooks at a later date.

Q1 Do you think that thought is controlled by language or language by thought?

Q2 Are there advantages to using foreign words in school textbooks?

UNIT 07

I got worried about you.

Unit Goals

Be able to talk about what happened to you.
Learn to use **"subject + got + adjective"**

01 Brainstorming

Exercise 1 Look at the pictures and find the phrases related to each picture. Then write the phrases under the pictures.

Words

- got promoted
- got sunburned
- got carsick
- got lost
- got tired
- got fired

got promoted

Exercise 2 Fill in the blanks with the answers above to complete the sentences.

A He _____ from his first job.

B I _____ to director.

C James _____ in the desert.

D They _____ of waiting.

E She _____ on the bus.

58 HighFive 1

02 Grammar

Grammar Focus

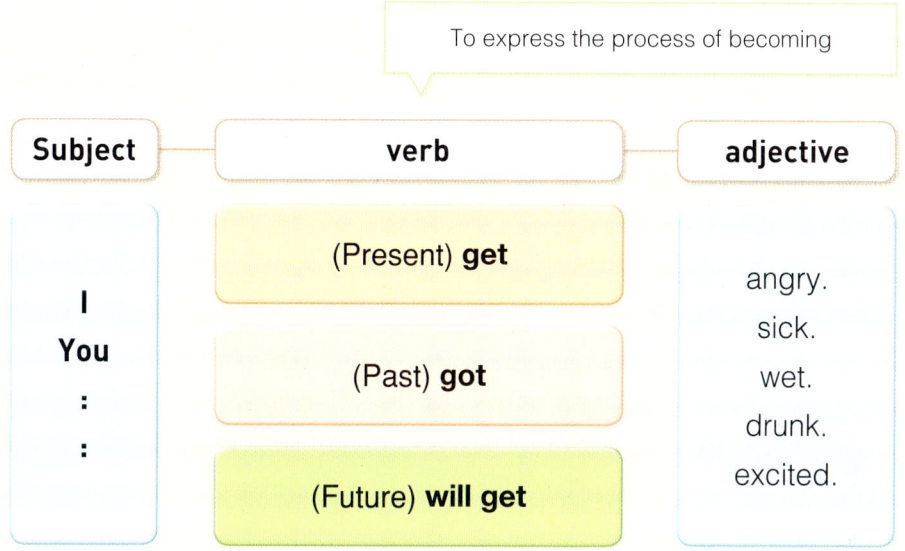

Exercise 3 Fill in the blanks with appropriate verb forms and/or adjectives from the boxes above.

A She got _____ about her new cell phone.

B I always _____ _____ fast.

C Mike got _____ in the rain.

D You will _____ _____ if you eat junk food.

E My boss _____ _____ because I was late for the meeting.

03 Vocabulary

Exercise 4 Look at the pictures and fill in the blanks with the appropriate words. Then practice with your partner.

| verbs | mad | hurt | worried | thirsty | married | divorced |

e.g.
A Do you _get mad_ when you lose games?
B Yes, I _get mad_ when I lose games.

A
A Did you get _____?
B Yes, I _____ _____ five years ago.

B
A Did you get _____ in the accident?
B Yes, I _____ _____ in the accident.

C
A When did you get _____?
B I _____ _____ last year.

D
A Did you get _____ about the test results?
B Yes, I _____ _____ about the test results.

E
A Do you get _____ after playing badminton?
B Yes, I _____ _____ after playing badminton.

04 Dialogue

Exercise 6 Look at the conversation. Fill in the blanks with the appropriate words from the box below. Then listen to the conversation and practice with your partner.

> mad   nervous   hurt   worried   tired

Chris: Sorry, I'm late Abigail.

Abigail: Chris! I heard about your car accident. Did you _____?

Chris: No, I didn't. I'm fine.

Abigail: Oh good. I got _worried_ about you.

Chris: Is Mr. Sanders in the meeting room?

Abigail: No, he left five minutes ago. He said he _____ of waiting.

Chris: Oh no! Did he _____ at me?

Abigail: Yes, a little bit.

Chris: Should I call him?

Abigail: Yes, you should.

Chris: Oh… I'm getting _____.

Unit 7 I got worried about you   61

05 Practice

Exercise 6 Look at the pictures and the tables. Then ask and answer the questions with your partner.

Name	Jun
Situation	- He is a team manager now. - Promoted

Ⓐ Jun is a team manager now.
Ⓑ Oh, did he get promoted?
Ⓐ Yes, he got promoted!

Name	Robin
Situation	- He worked overtime every night. - Tired of working

Ⓐ
Ⓑ
Ⓐ

Name	Terry
Situation	- She fell off her bicycle on the weekend. - Hurt

Ⓐ
Ⓑ
Ⓐ

Name	Luke
Situation	- His GPS didn't work this morning. - Lost

Ⓐ
Ⓑ
Ⓐ

06 Application

Exercise 7 Look at the questions and write your answers. Then practice with your partner.

e.g.
Q Did you get married?
A Yes, I _got married_ three years ago.

A
Q Did you get paid today?
A _____.

B
Q Did you get tired of your commute?
A _____.

C
Q Did you get worried about your job performance?
A _____.

07 Discussion

Exercise 8 Read the following story and fill in the blanks with the given words. Share your ideas with your partner and present them to the whole class.

① procedures   ② compliment   ③ appearance   ④ injections   ⑤ considered

Young and old flock to anti-aging care

When someone says that a person has a "baby face," it is __A__ a __B__. It says that someone is younger than their real age. In today's society, people are trying to stay young forever. Korea ranks number 3 in the world in plastic surgery. However, many Koreans are moving away from surgery and going towards __C__ that give them a much younger __D__. Many are going with Botox injections, which helps to give the skin a more youthful look. In 2015, 279,019 Botox __E__ were performed in Korea. While such injections are usually for people in their 40s or 50s, people in their 20s and 30s are getting them, too.

There are many ways a person stay looking youthful. However, the procedures are often quite expensive. Skin care can cost between 100,000 and 150,000 won. Botox injections can cost between 300,000 to 2 million won. Yet, despite the costs, it appears that many people of all age groups are seeking natural looks and anti-aging procedures are a popular way to do it.

Q1 Do you want people to tell you that you look younger? Is it a compliment for everyone? Do you think plastic surgery is necessary? If not, why?

Q2 At what age do you think your skin will start to show signs of age?

08 UNIT

It smells great!

Unit Goals

Be able to talk about the five senses.
Learn to use **"subject + sense verb + adjective"**

01 Brainstorming

Exercise 1 Look at the adjectives in the middle and place them into the appropriate circles.

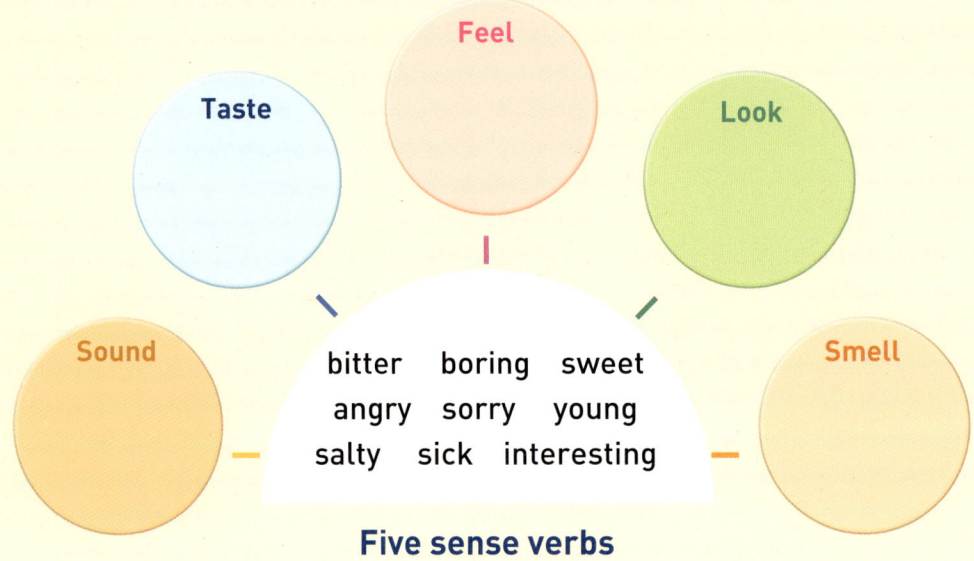

bitter boring sweet
angry sorry young
salty sick interesting

Five sense verbs

Exercise 2 Fill in the blanks with appropriate sense verbs.

A This chicken　*tastes*　salty.

B I　_____　sick today.

C Something　_____　fishy.

D Dark chocolate　_____　bitter.

E You　_____　very angry.

02 Grammar

Grammar Focus

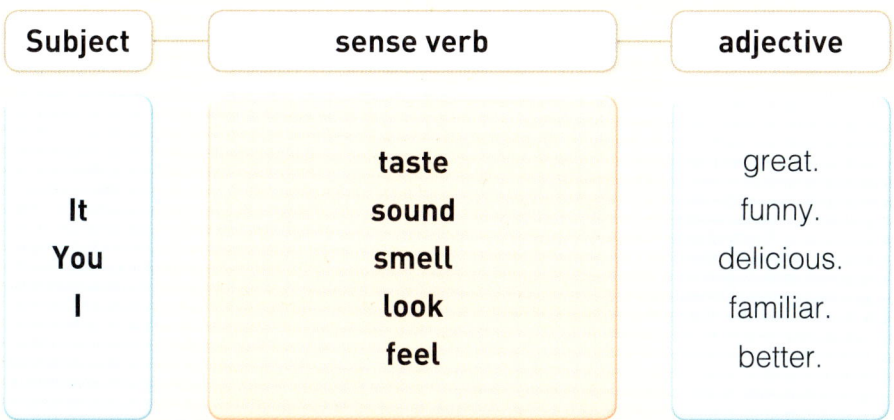

Exercise 3 Fill in the blanks with appropriate verbs and/or adjectives from the boxes above. Then add your own sentences. (Answers may vary)

A It tastes *delicious* .

B You look _____ .

C I _____ better.

D You _____ familiar.

E It _____ funny.

D It smells _____ .

03 Vocabulary

Exercise 4 Look at the pictures and fill in the blanks with the appropriate words. Then practice with your partner.

| verbs | sour   comfortable   sorry   ridiculous   terrible   tired |

e.g.
- A: How do you feel today?
- B: I feel very _tired_.

A
- A: How does the orange taste?
- B: It tastes _____.

B
- A: Jake got fired from his job.
- B: Oh, I feel _____ for him.

C
- A: My boss said it was my mistake.
- B: It sounds _____.

D
- A: How does the sock smell?
- B: This smells _____.

E
- A: How do you feel about Jenny?
- B: I feel very _____ with her.

04 Dialogue

Exercise 6 Look at the conversation. Fill in the blanks with the appropriate words from the box below. Then listen to the conversation and practice with your partner.

> look   great   tastes   delicious   better   sound

Vicky: Let's have coffee here. It smells _great_!

Jay: _____ good.

Vicky: (In the café) What do you want to drink? An Americano, as usual?

Jay: Look! A new drink is available! It's a caramel-flavored cold brew... It sounds _____!

Vicky: It _____ better than an Americano.

Jay: (After a couple of sips) Hmm, it _____ good.

Vicky: It looks _____, too. I will try one next time.

Unit8 It smells great! 69

05 Practice

Exercise 6 Ask and answer the questions about the people in the pictures.

What happened?
Tim is watching a movie, but it's not interesting.
➡ Tim feels bored.
➡ Tim feels bad about the movie.

What happened?
Ivan failed the job interview and he is not happy.
➡
➡

What happened?
Valerie is on a blind date and she really likes him.
➡
➡

What happened?
Adrian had an argument with his coworker yesterday.
➡
➡

06 Application

Exercise 7 Give your answers.

e.g.
Q What do you think about moving to a new city?
A _It sounds great_ or _That sounds hard_ .

A
Q What do you think about very spicy food?
A _____ .

B
Q What do you think about meeting new people?
A _____ .

C
Q What do you think about travelling alone?
A _____ .

Unit8 It smells great!

07 Discussion

Exercise 8 Read the following story and fill in the blanks with the given words. Share your ideas with your partner and present them to the whole class.

① influence ② features ③ attempt ④ bans ⑤ launched ⑥ demonstrating

Chinese Newspaper launches English app to expand influence

The People's Daily, the newspaper of China's ruling Communist Party, __A__ an English-language application in an __B__ to increase China's international __C__. This comes at a time when China's president is interested in __D__ China's growing international influence. Government officials hope the English mobile app will promote the theories and philosophy of China's Communist Party and good stories coming out of China. The People's Daily is not just a newspaper, but also a website that __E__ articles in eight languages.

In addition to the People's Daily, China also has many international news channels that bring news from China to the rest of the world in many languages. All these resources are part of China's effort to spread the word of its president and the good things about China. Yet, while China seeks to spread news about what is happening in the country, it is very careful about what news it lets in from the outside world. The Chinese government closely controls all information that enters the country and __F__ foreign websites like the New York Times. The control of the internet and the different security measures China uses are often called "The Great Firewall."

Q1 China is a country which strictly controls the press. What are the advantages and disadvantages of launching this app about China?

Q2 What have you heard about CCTV, the People's Daily, and Xinhua? Are you confident in the news that the Chinese media releases?

09 UNIT

It has been 7 years since I saw you.

Unit Goals

Be able to talk about how long it has been since you did something.
Learn to use **"it + has + been+ ... + since + I + past verb + (noun)"**

01 Brainstorming

Exercise 1 Write the appropriate words under the pictures.

| study English   attend a graduation ceremony   get up in the morning |
| have a meal   meet your school friends   read a book |

Exercise 2 Ask and answer the questions based on the answers from above. Then practice with your partner.

e.g.
Q How long has it been since you've met your high school friends?
A *I haven't met my high school friends for a year*.

A
Q How long has it been since you've read a book?
A _____.

B
Q How long has it been since you've eaten?
A _____.

C
Q How long has it been since you've studied English?
A _____.

74 HighFive 1

02 Grammar

Grammar Focus

It/has been	duration	since	Subject + past verb + (noun)
It has (It's) been	7 years 4 months 10 years 12 hours 3 days	since	I saw my uncle. I smoked. I used this chair. I had breakfast. I bought this bag.

Exercise 3 Read the conversation and answer the following questions.

e.g.
- Q How long has it been since you left America, James?
- A It has been 7 years since I left America.

A
- Q How long has it been since you smoked?
- A _____.

B
- Q How long has it been since you bought a new bag?
- A _____.

C
- Q How long has it been since you used this chair?
- A _____.

Unit9 It has been 7 years since I saw you

03 Vocabulary

Exercise 4 Duration adjectives describe the length of time for which something happens. Match the words on the left with the meanings on the right.

historical	too long
endless	latest
lengthy	vast, huge
temporary	lasting for a short time
up to date	to have no end
tremendous	concerned with events of the past

Exercise 5 Fill the blanks with the words from Exercise 4.

A. Researchers have put _____ time and effort into AI technologies.

B. This meeting seems to be _____, but it has been only 10 minutes since the meeting started.

C. It was just a _____ contract, but I'm satisfied with my paycheck.

D. The _____ lecture is making me sleepy. It has already been 2 hours!

04 Dialogue

Exercise 6 Look at the conversation. Fill in the blanks with the appropriate words from the box below. Then listen to the conversation and practice with your partner.

> been   since   should   has been   have   be   It's

Jenny: Look, who's here! It's Alex!

Alex: Wow! Jenny! It _has been_ 7 years _____ I saw you.

Jenny: What brought you here?

Alex: I came back to Korea to work. I have _____ here for 3 years.

Jenny: That's great! How's your wife, Jessica? Do you have kids?

Alex: I have a son, now. He's just _____ born!

Jenny: Congratulation! We _____ have dinner sometime. We have so many things to catch up on!

Alex: My wife will _____ excited to see you. _____ been a few months since we've met any of our friends.

Unit9 It has been 7 years since I saw you

05 Practice

Exercise 7 Think about things you haven't. How long has it been since you did them?

Things you haven't done for a while	For how long?

Exercise 8 Have a conversation with the given information.

Things you haven't done recently	When
Go swimming	3 years ago
Call your mom	a month ago
Get a new job	a year ago
Practice Chinse	6 months

e.g.
- Q Do you go swimming these days?
- A No, I don't. It has been 3 years since I went swimming.

A
- Q Do you often talk with your mom? When was the last time you called her?
- A No, I don't. _____.

B
- Q Did you get a new job?
- A Yes, I did. _____.

C
- Q Do you practice Chinese?
- A No, I don't. _____.

78 HighFive 1

06 Application

Exercise 9 People make plans for the future all the time. For example, I will lose weight, or I will be a fluent English speaker. In 5 years from now, do you think you will be doing things you have resolved to do? Suppose in the future you're writing about what you have been doing for the last five years. What would you write?

February, 7, 2030

It's been 1 year since I last smoked
I have studied English for
the last two years.

February, 7, 2030

07 Discussion

Exercise 10 Read the following story and fill in the blanks with the given words. Share your ideas with your partner and present them to the whole class.

① recognition ② significant ③ identifying ④ artificially ⑤ accurately ⑥ task

A.I that can make its own A.I

Researchers have dreamed for a long time of __A_____ intelligent machines that can make other A.I. machines. Now the dream is becoming reality. Technology company SearchEng has recently created a program called Self ML. Machine Learning, or ML, is a computer program that learns a certain __B_____ on its own by looking at data. Self ML is a machine-learning program that will learn to create other machine-learning programs.

Many companies see this as the future of the technology industry. Already, companies are developing tools that will make it easier for a computer program to create its own AI for image and voice __C_____. However, making an ML program is very different from building a website or a smartphone application. ML requires __D_____ math and many versions before it works well. SearchEng has created a program that can build other ML programs by itself whiles also learning which methods are successful and which are not. Such programs could be used for services like __E_____ objects in photos more __F_____ than a program made by humans. Some believe that the same methods could be used for other tasks, like speech recognition or machine translations.

Q1 What are the advantages and disadvantages of A.I.?

Q2 Why do you think scientists are developing A.I.?

UNIT 10

He talks too much.

Unit Goals

Be able to talk about how something is done.
Learn to use **"subject + verb + adverb"**

01 Brainstorming

Exercise 1 Guess the meaning of the verbs in the box and write each word under a picture.

Verbs

- sneeze
- sweat
- laugh
- smile
- snore
- yawn

snore

Exercise 2 Fill in the blanks. Then practice with your partner.

A I ___snore___ a lot.

B I _____ a lot.

C I _____ a lot.

D I _____ a lot.

E I don't _____ a lot.

F I don't _____ a lot.

02 Grammar

Grammar Focus

Exercise 3 Fill in the blanks with the appropriate words from the boxes above. (Answers may vary)

A I _sleep_ too much.

B The baby _____ every night.

C He drinks _____ .

D She coughs _____ .

E You _____ a lot.

F I don't eat snacks _____ .

03 Vocabulary

Exercise 4 Look at the pictures and fill in the blanks with the appropriate words from the box. Then practice with your partner.

| verbs | talk   smile   stretch   cry   dance |

e.g.
A Do you _talk_ a lot?
B Yes, I ___talk all the time___.

A
A Does he _____ a lot?
B Yes / No, he _____.

B
A Do you _____ a lot?
B Yes / No, I _____.

C
A Does she _____ a lot?
B Yes / No, she _____.

D
A Do you _____ a lot?
B Yes / No, I _____.

84 HighFive 1

04 Dialogue

Exercise 6 Look at the conversation. Fill in the blanks with the appropriate words from the box below. Then listen to the conversation and practice with your partner.

> sleep   talk   complain   drink

Charles: Welcome to the marketing department. Let me introduce our team members.

Stefani: Thanks.

Charles: The guy over there is Mike. He's nice, but he's not quiet. He ___talks___ too much.

Stefani: I see.

Charles: That is Amy. She's very smart, but she _____ all the time. She doesn't like many things.

Stefani: Oh…

Charles: He's James, our team leader. He _____ a lot. He's a heavy drinker.

Stefani: Hmm…

Charles: I'm Charles. I usually go to bed very late, so I _____ in the office all day.

Stefani: What?

Unit10 He talks too much   85

05 Practice

Exercise 6 Look at the pictures and given information. Then make full sentences with the information and the appropriate adverbs. Share your answers with your partner. (Answers may vary)

e.g.

Who	Luke
What	Dizzy
Why	He drank

➡ Luke feels dizzy because he drank too much.

A

Who	Claire
What	Tired
Why	Her husband snored

➡ _____

B

Who	Daisy
What	Annoyed
Why	The dog next door barked

➡ _____

06 Application

Exercise 7 Give your answers to the questions. Then practice with your partner.

e.g.
Q Do you talk a lot?
A Yes, I talk all day.

A
Q Do you snore all night?
A _____.

B
Q Do you drink too much?
A _____.

C
Q Do you sweat a lot?
A _____.

D
Q Do you complain all the time?
A _____.

07 Discussion

Exercise 8 Read the following story and fill in the blanks with the given words. Share your ideas with your partner and present them to the whole class.

① firearm   ② spike   ③ concerning   ④ stability   ⑤ bump   ⑥ unintentional

Gun deaths rising in the US

Gun deaths in the United States have risen to 12 people per 100,000. This increase comes after a long period of __A__. The report was completed by the Centers for Disease Control's Health Statistics Center and shows a sharp increase this year, which is __B__ for some at the CDC. 33,000 people die every year in __C__ -related deaths according to the CDC. However, the new report comes after a series of mass shootings in the United States, which has sparked discussion of gun violence and new attempts at gun control.

Although mass shootings only count for two percent of total gun deaths, they have an outsized impact because of news reports. The mass shootings have an effect on people because the victims and locations of the shootings are places many people like to visit, like night clubs and music concerts. Suicides count for about 60 percent of all gun deaths in America, with murders counting for 36 percent. Deaths related to police shootings or __D__ actions are 1.3 percent. The CDC report has noted that America has gone more than twenty years without any improvement in the number of deaths related to gun violence. Some officials hope that the __E__ in violence is a small __F__ and that no further increases will come.

Q1 Do you think the U.S needs to reconsider the legality of firearm possessio?

Q2 What policies could reduce the gun violence? What about education about gun safety, smart gun technology, or ending legal immunity for gun manufacturers?

I couldn't sleep last night.

Unit Goals

Be able to talk about situations.
Learn to use **"subject + verb + adverb phrase"**

01 Brainstorming

Exercise 1 Guess the meaning of the verbs in the box and write each word under the appropriate picture.

Verbs

- close
- arrive
- appear
- fly
- stay
- open

stay | _____ | _____

_____ | _____ | _____

Exercise 2 Fill in the blanks with verbs above. Then match the sentences on the left with appropriate adverbial phrases on the right.

A　I _____stayed_____　　　　　　　　　• in the evening

B　The restaurant _____　　　　• at the station

C　The store _____　　　　　　• at home

D　She _____　　　　　　　　• at night

E　Airplanes _____　　　　　　• in the morning

F　A ghost _____　　　　　　　• in the sky

02 Grammar

Grammar Focus

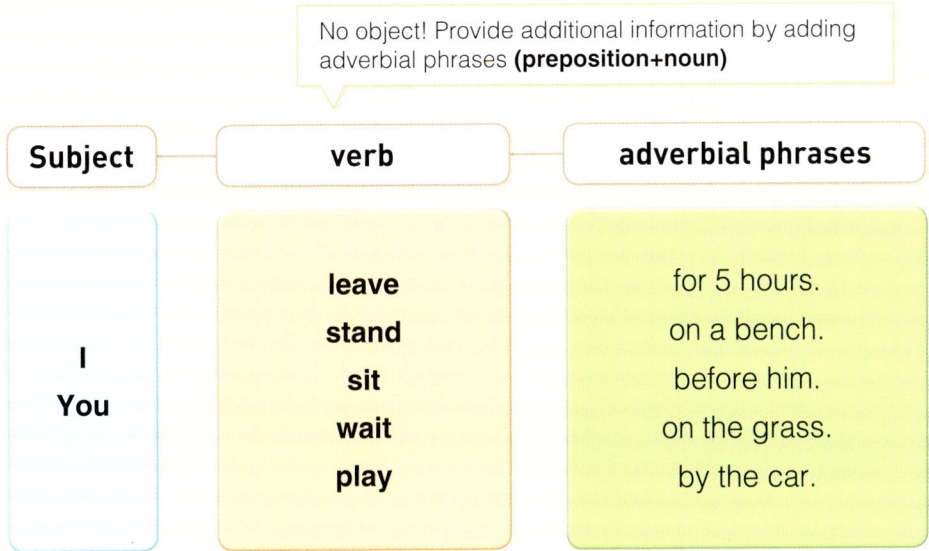

Exercise 3 Fill in the blanks with appropriate adverbial phrases from the box above. Then practice with your partner.

A I left   *before him*   .

B The police officer is standing _____ .

C She waited _____ .

D The dog is playing _____ .

E I sat _____ .

03 Vocabulary

Exercise 4 Look at the conversations and fill in the blanks with the appropriate verb forms from the box. Then practice with your partner.

| verbs | last   exist   live   come   depart |

e.g.
- **Zack** Where did you _live_ in 2015?
- **Gloria** I _lived_ in China.

A
- **Baker** How long does the battery _____?
- **Brittany** It _____ for seven hours.

B
- **Justin** When does the train _____?
- **Ryder** It _____ at 8 o'clock in the morning.

C
- **Maria** How did you _____ here?
- **Howard** I _____ in my car.

D
- **Niki** Does the word _____ in Korean?
- **Paris** No, it doesn't _____ in Korean.

04 Dialogue

Exercise 6 Look at the conversation. Fill in the blanks with the appropriate words from the box below. Then listen to the conversation and practice with your partner.

> bark   sit   study   arrive   sleep

Kevin: Vicky, are you all right? You look tired.

Vicky: I couldn't _sleep_ last night.

Kevin: Why?

Vicky: I _____ for 3 hours.

Kevin: Did you sleep after that?

Vicky: No, I didn't. My dog _____ all night.

Kevin: Oh…

Vicky: And then, my husband _____ home from his business trip.

Kevin: What did you do after that?

Vicky: I was _____ on the couch until 6 o'clock in the morning.

Kevin: I think you need a wp of strong coffee!

Unit11 I couldn't sleep last night

05 Practice

Exercise 6 Look at the pictures, given verbs (a), and adverb phrases (b). Then match the verbs with appropriate adverb phrases. Share your answers with your partner. (Answers may vary)

(a) walk   run   eat   respond

(b) before class   to my email   on the street   to the station

e.g. She _____walks on the street_____.

A She _____.

B They _____.

C She _____.

94 HighFive 1

06 Application

Exercise 7 Give your answers to the questions. Then practice with your partner.

e.g.
Q Do you sleep after midnight?
A _No, I don't sleep after midnight_. Or _I sleep before midnight_.

A
Q Do you **walk to the bus station** in the morning?
A _____.

B
Q Do you **eat at night**?
A _____.

C
Q Do you **stay at home** on weekends?
A _____.

D
Q Do you like to **spend time with your friends**?
A _____.

07 Discussion

Exercise 8 Read the following story and fill in the blanks with the given words. Share your ideas with your partner and present them to the whole class.

① chopping ② disappearance ③ nutrients ④ storage ⑤ packaging

Can packaged vegetables lose vitamins?

Food scientists say that green vegetables have vitamins that can be lost through __A__ for the markets. Vitamins C and B can be lost through washing and __B__ as they are packaged or if they sit in the refrigerator for too long. One study has shown spinach loses half its vitamin B after eight days in the refrigerator. However, lettuce maintained most of its vitamin B even if kept in the refrigerator. But, most vitamins and nutrients are not lost. Vitamins A, E, K and minerals like iron and calcium remain long after washing or long periods of __C__. But vitamin C is a problem. A recent study has shown that spinach lost more vitamin C than any other green vegetable. It lost about 80 percent after just three days of storage. In contrast, watercress kept nearly 60 percent of its vitamin C after 10 days. Researchers say that the __D__ of vitamin C is not a serious health risk. This is because most people get enough vitamin C from other parts of their diet.

It is important to remember, researchers say, that people should focus on eating lots of fruits and vegetables. If people are worried about their __E__, they should eat their vegetables when they are fresh.

Q1 What do you do to maintain the freshness of fruits and vegetables at home?

Q2 How do you get enough vitamins? Do you try to eat enough fruits and vegetables? Or do you take vitamin pills?

UNIT 12

I didn't attend the meeting.

Unit Goals

Be able to talk about meetings.
Learn to use **"subject + verb + noun"**

01 Brainstorming

Exercise 1 Look at the verbs in the two boxes, (a) and (b), and find the difference between them.

(a)
I **go** to church on Sundays.
She **looks** at the pictures.
The river **runs** into the sea.
He **waited** for a bus
I **applied** for the job.

(b)
She **married** a Korean guy.
I will **call** you tomorrow.
I **attend** a meeting.
She **entered** the university.
He **asked** a question.

Exercise 2 Fill in the blanks with appropriate verbs from the box(b).

A I _____ you earlier.

B She _____ a lawyer last year.

C I _____ classes in the afternoon.

D He _____ me to work this weekend.

E Please _____ the room one by one.

98 HighFive 1

02 Grammar

Grammar Focus

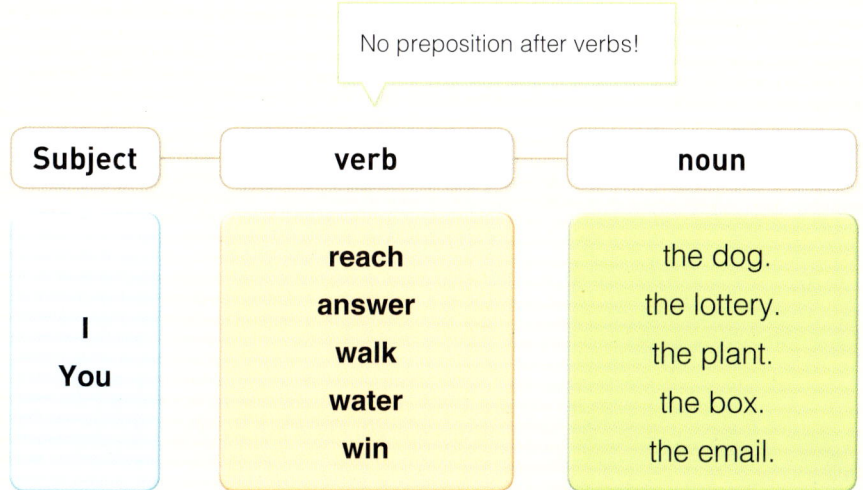

Exercise 3   Fill in the blanks with appropriate words from the box above. Then share your answers with your partner.

A   I _____ my dog every morning.

B   You should _____ the plant every day.

C   I didn't answer _____ yet.

D   She won _____ yesterday!

E   He can't _____ the box on the shelf.

03 Vocabulary

Exercise 4   Look at the conversations and fill in the blanks with appropriate forms of verbs in the box. Then practice with your partner.

| verbs | resemble | meet | lack | discuss | contact |

A
- A: Do u want to have a coffee after work today?
- B: I should _____ my client this evening.

B
- A: Did you _____ Ms. Harrison?
- B: Yes, I did yesterday.

C
- A: I found an error with our new product.
- B: Let's _____ the problem today.

D
- A: I don't understand why you don't like Gerald.
- B: He _____ common sense.

E
- A: The baby _____ its father.
- B: No, he looks like his mother.

100 HighFive 1

04 Dialogue

Exercise 6 Look at the conversation. Fill in the blanks with the appropriate words from the box below. Then listen to the conversation and practice with your partner.

> meet   contact   discuss   attend   answer

Jill: Hey Jay, I didn't see you in the staff meeting today.

Jay: I didn't ___*attend*___ the meeting.

Jill: Why?

Jay: I had a family emergency this morning.

Jill: Oh, I'm sorry to hear that. Did you _____ the manager before that?

Jay: I tried, but he didn't _____ my call.

Jill: Hmm, he seemed angry.

Jay: What should I do?

Jill: You should _____ him to _____ this problem.

Jay: OK, I will do that now.

Unit12 I didn't attend the meeting

05 Practice

Exercise 6 Look at the pictures and key words. Then ask and answer questions about the pictures by using the key words and appropriate verbs.

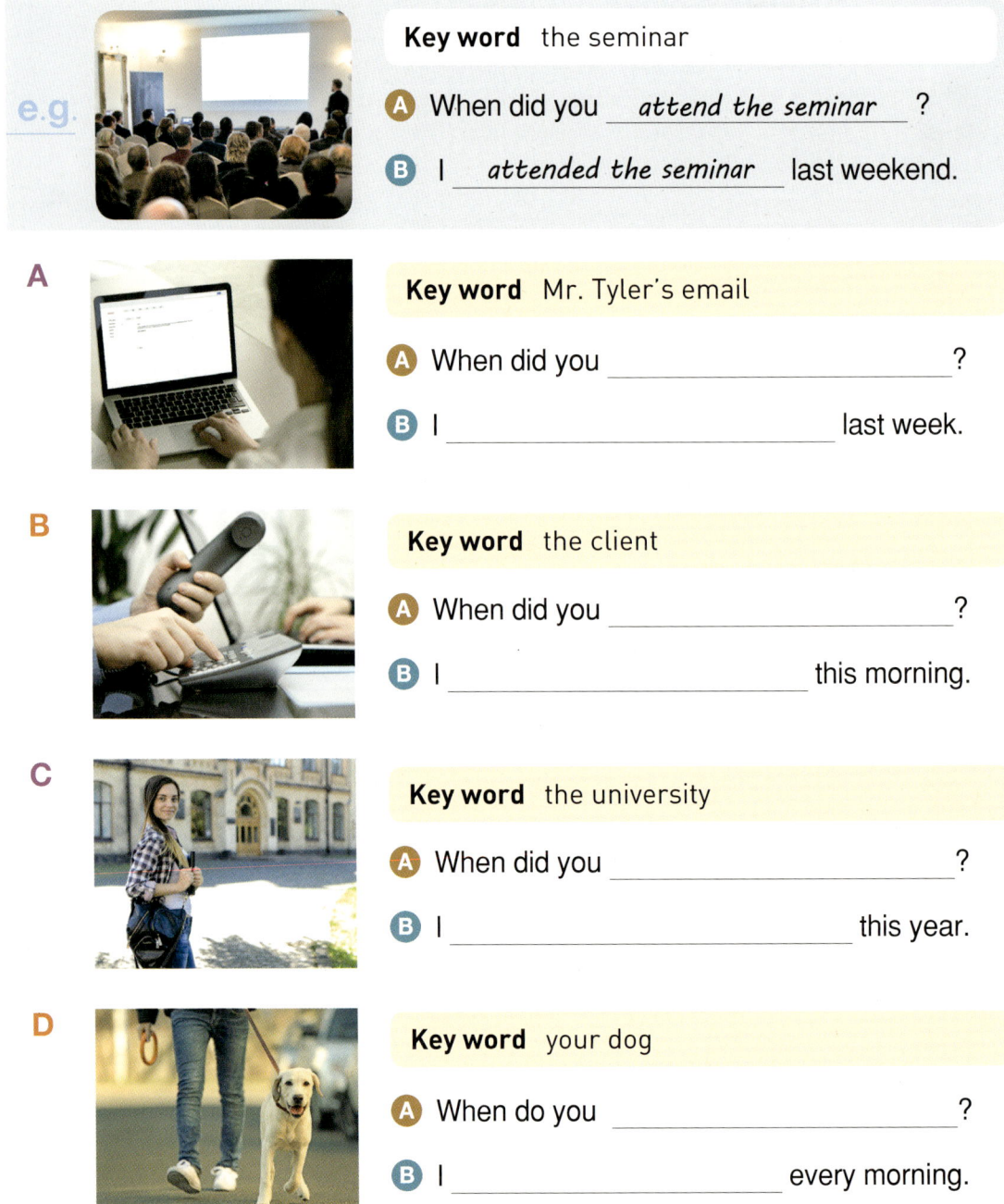

e.g.

Key word the seminar

Ⓐ When did you ___attend the seminar___ ?

Ⓑ I ___attended the seminar___ last weekend.

A

Key word Mr. Tyler's email

Ⓐ When did you _____ ?

Ⓑ I _____ last week.

B

Key word the client

Ⓐ When did you _____ ?

Ⓑ I _____ this morning.

C

Key word the university

Ⓐ When did you _____ ?

Ⓑ I _____ this year.

D

Key word your dog

Ⓐ When do you _____ ?

Ⓑ I _____ every morning.

06 Application

Exercise 7 Look at the questions and give your answers to the questions. Then practice with your partner.

e.g.
Q Did you marry a Korean woman?
A Yes, I did. *I married a Korean woman* .

A
Q When did you call your best friend?
A _____.

B
Q When did you enter the university?
A _____.

C
Q Do you attend a staff meeting every week?
A _____.

D
Q Do you answer calls at night?
A _____.

Unit12 I didn't attend the meeting

07 Discussion

Exercise 8 Read the following story and fill in the blanks with the given words. Share your ideas with your partner and present them to the whole class.

① chilled ② grueling ③ sore ④ debated ⑤ cool

Muscles get better with heat after exercise.

A new study finds that muscles get better after exercising if they are warmed and not __A_____. Many athletes have __B_____ for a long time about the best way to help __C_____ muscles after a long and tiring exercise. Some athletes prefer to do icing, where they __D_____ their muscles. Others prefer

medicine to help with aches and pains. However, many studies have shown that cooling muscles or using painkillers doesn't help stop pain. One reason that muscles get tired so easily is because of a loss of the muscle's glycogen, a carbohydrate that gives muscles energy. Carbohydrates are like food for muscles. When the muscle loses glycogen, they become weak, tired, and sore.

Researchers in Sweden performed a test to see if warming muscles after exercise helped them get any strength back. Five athletes were tested. They were put through a series of __E_____ exercises. Afterwards their muscles were warmed with long cuffs while the athletes ate foods that had carbohydrates. The scientists discovered that warming the muscles helped in getting more glycogen in to the muscles, which helped them get better faster.

Q1 Have you used a pain relief patch? There are many types of pain relief medications like ointments, gels, and sprays. What do you think is the fastest and most effective way to relieve pain?

Q2 Do you know any stretches or simple exercises for pain relief?

UNIT 13

I ask him for an autograph.

Unit Goals

Be able to talk about what you ask for.
Learn to use **"subject + verb + noun + for + noun"**

01 Brainstorming

Exercise 1 Look at the two boxes, (a) and (b), and match the verbs on the left with the appropriate nouns on the right. Share your answers with your partner. (Verbs can be used more than once)

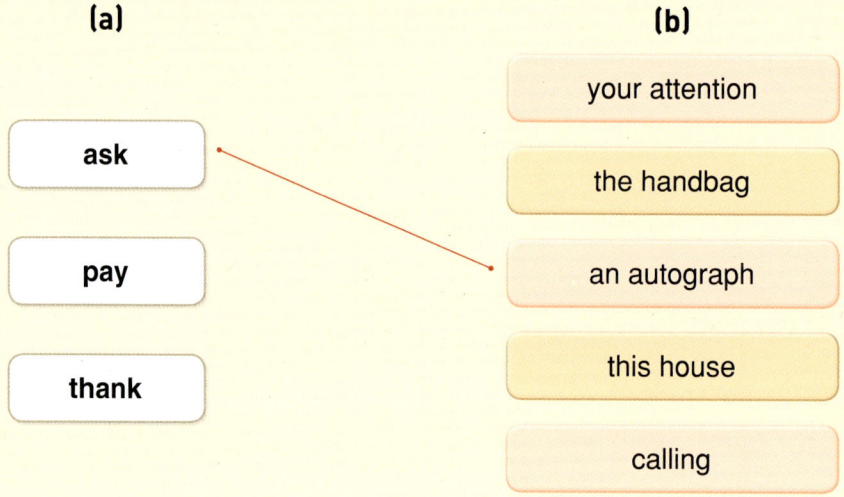

Exercise 2 Fill in the blanks- Connect the verbs and nouns above by using a preposition "for".

A I _asked_ him **for** _an autograph_ .

B I _____ 100 dollars **for** _____ .

C _Thank_ you **for** _____ .

D _____ a lot of money **for** _____ .

E _____ you **for** _____ .

106 HighFive 1

02 Grammar

Grammar Focus

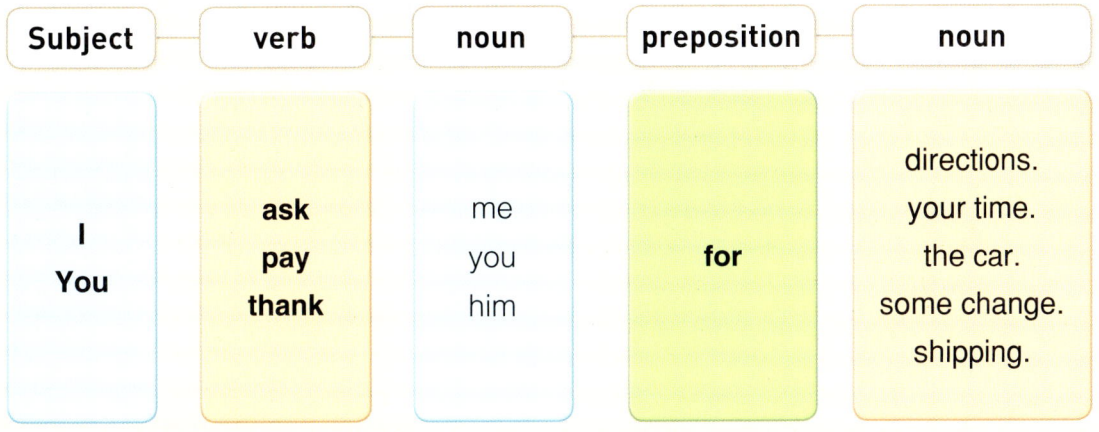

Subject	verb	noun	preposition	noun
I You	ask pay thank	me you him	for	directions. your time. the car. some change. shipping.

Exercise 3 Fill in the blanks by using the key words. Then share your answers with your partner.

A Key word
ask, directions

I _asked_ her _for directions_ .

B Key word
thank, your time

_____ you _____ .

C Key word
shipping, pay

I _____ 5 dollars _____ .

D Key word
some change, ask

She _____ him _____ .

E Key word
pay, cash

He _____ the car.

Unit13 I ask him for an autograph

03 Vocabulary

Exercise 4 Look at the conversations and fill in the blanks with appropriate words from the box. Then practice with your partner.

Verbs & Nouns	ask pay thank coffee
	your help new dress the ride

A

Mona What did you ask her?

Brian I _____ her for water.

B

Lee _____ you for _____.

Chuck My pleasure!

C

Young Wow, your _____ looks very expensive.

Jennifer Actually, I _____ 50 dollars for this.

D

Stefan _____ you for _____.

Erin You're welcome.

E

Rob You ordered a tea, right?

Gary No, I _____ you for _____.

108 HighFive 1

04 Dialogue

Exercise 6 Look at the conversation. Fill in the blanks with the appropriate words from the box below. Then listen to the conversation and practice with your partner.

> service fees   an autograph   the ticket   coming

Peter: Hey, Jenny. How was the concert last night?

Jenny: It was awesome! I met the singer!

Peter: Did you take a photo with him?

Jenny: Yes! Then I asked him _for an autograph_.

Peter: Wow! Did you get it?

Jenny: Of course! He told me "Thank you for _____." It was an amazing experience.

Peter: How much was the concert ticket?

Jenny: I _____ 100 dollars for _____.

Peter: That isn't too bad.

Jenny: But I paid 50 dollars for _____.

Peter: Hmm…

Unit13 I ask him for an autograph

05 Practice

Exercise 6 Look at the pictures and key words. Then ask and answer about the pictures using the key words and appropriate verbs.

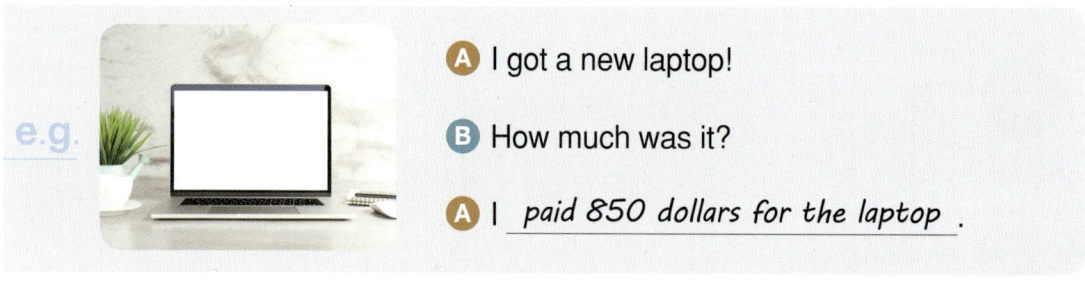

e.g.
- **A** I got a new laptop!
- **B** How much was it?
- **A** I _paid 850 dollars for the laptop_ .

A
- **A** Here is your steak.
- **B** Um, I _____ .
- **A** Oh, I'm so sorry.

B
- **A** I heard you bought a new house.
- **B** Yes! I _____ .
- **A** Wow, that's very expensive.

C
- **A** Did you have a good time today?
- **B** Yes! _____ .
- **A** My pleasure.

06 Application

Exercise 7 Look at the picture and questions below. Then practice with your partner by asking and answering the questions. (Answers may vary)

e.g.

a car

Q How much did you pay for your car? **A** *I paid 10,000 dollars for the car.*

Q What did you ask the seller for? **A** *I asked him for a red car.*

shoes

Ask your partner about his or her shoes.

Q   **A**

Q   **A**

07 Discussion

Exercise 8 Read the following story and fill in the blanks with the given words. Share your ideas with your partner and present them to the whole class.

① crisis ② persuading ③ offensive ④ refuse ⑤ vast

Social media site strong against all problems

While many advertising companies __A__ to do business with social media sites that show __B__ content, Facebook seems to be different. Advertising companies still use Facebook no matter what problems the company has or what offensive content they show. This is because of the reach that Facebook has. Billions of people all over the world use Facebook, which offers advertising companies a chance to use the __C__ audience to reach billions of new customers with their ads. From selling cars, or cosmetics to __D__ people to vote for a political candidate, Facebook has the reach and influence that many companies want when selling their products. Facebook is very good at targeting different groups and feeding them advertisements that that group particularly likes. When a social media site is going through a particular __E__, advertising companies will pull their ads and put them on a similar site. However, for Facebook that is not the case. There is no other social media platform like Facebook that has the same reach and persuasive power. If an advertising company pulls their ads from Facebook, they risk losing money and new customers.

Q1 Do you agree that social media is the best way for companies to advertise and promote their goods and services? What are the advantages and disadvantages of social media advertising?

Q2 Do you know a specific company that makes good use of social media for its advertising?

UNIT 14

Did you send me a text?

Unit Goals

Be able to talk about what you did.
Learn to use **"subject + verb + noun + noun"**

01 Brainstorming

Exercise 1 Look at the pictures and match them with the appropriate verbs and nouns in the box.

| verb | give   send   teach   make |

| nouns | a text message   a dinner   a call   a lesson |

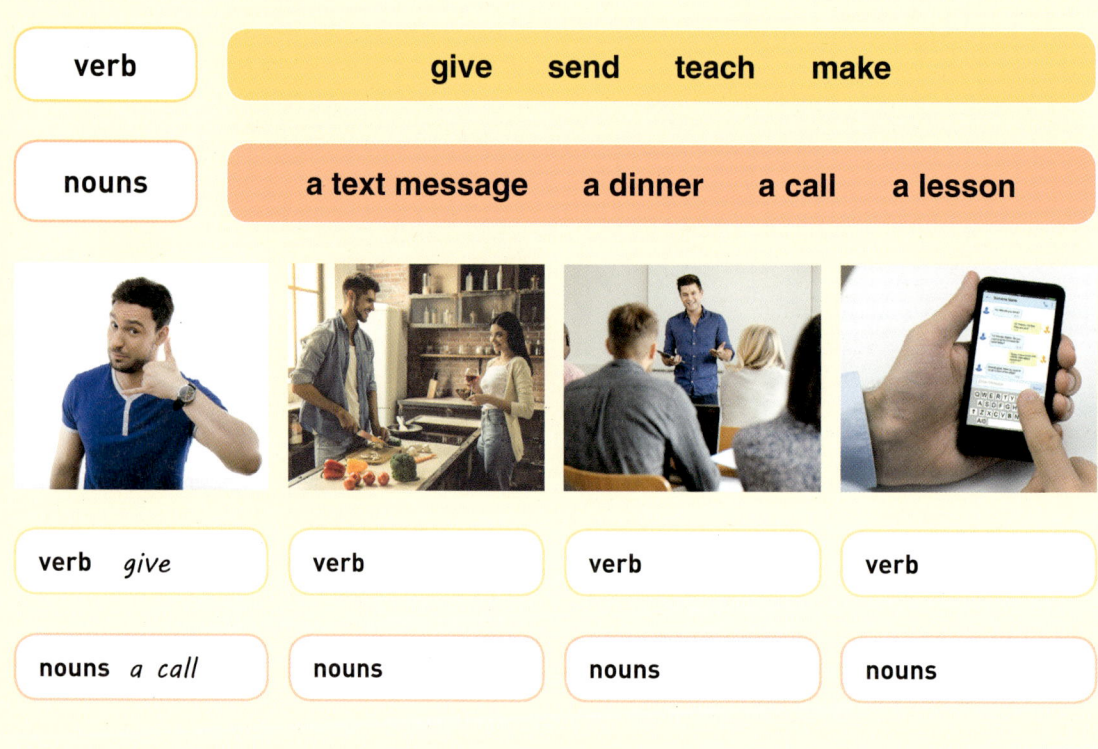

| verb *give* | verb | verb | verb |
| nouns *a call* | nouns | nouns | nouns |

Exercise 2 Fill in the blanks. Then practice with your partner.

A He *gave* me *a call* .

B He _____ her _____ .

C He _____ us _____ .

D He _____ me _____ .

02 Grammar

Grammar Focus

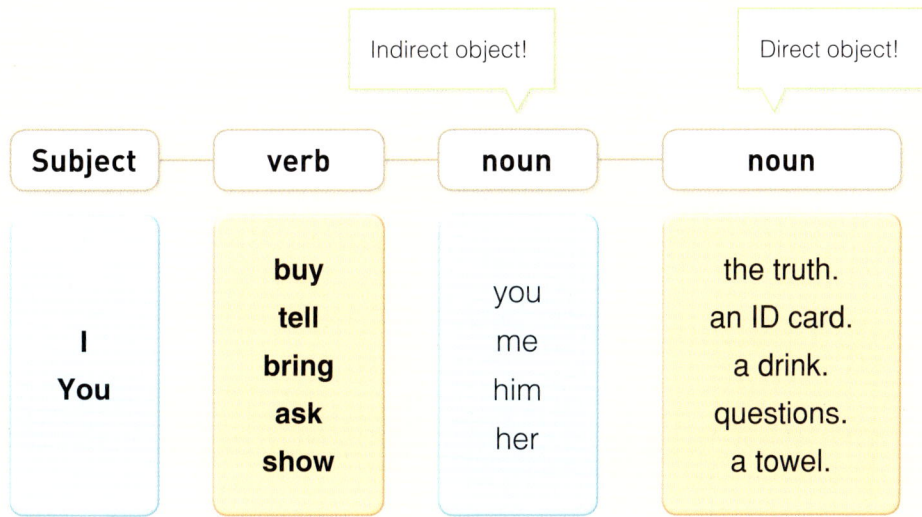

Exercise 3 Fill in the blanks with the appropriate verbs or nouns from the boxes above. Then share your answers with your partner.

A She _____ me the truth.

B I asked him some _____ .

C The janitor _____ him his ID card.

D I brought her _____ .

E He _____ me a drink.

03 Vocabulary

Exercise 4 Look at the pictures and conversations. Fill in the blanks with appropriate words from the box. Then practice with your partner.

Verbs & Nouns	lend give make read buy a discount a secondhand car money a promise this letter

e.g.

Joanna Your suit looks nice and expensive.

Tim The seller _gave me a discount_ .

A

Henry You got a new car!

Danny My dad _____ me _____ .

B

Han Can you _____ _____ some _____ ?

Aiden Sure. How much do you need?

C

Dona Can you _____ me _____ ?

Aiden Sure, grandma.

D

Dona He _____ _____ a promise.

Aiden You know him. He never keeps a promise.

04 Dialogue

Exercise 6 Look at the conversation. Fill in the blanks with the appropriate words from the box below. Then listen to the conversation and practice with your partner.

| ask   more questions   show   me   a presentation   give   how to prepare |

Ben: Hey, did you _send_ me _a text_ ?

Jun: Yes, we will have a staff meeting in an hour.

Ben: What? Why?

Jun: Our boss _____ us more work.

Ben: Oh no…

Jun: And he will _____ us lots _____ about our project during the meeting.

Ben: Ok…

Jun: One more thing, you should give him _____.

Ben: I think I need to prepare for the meeting now.

Jun: I will _____ you _____.

Ben: Thank you for your help!

Unit14 Did you send me a text? **117**

05 Practice

Exercise 6 Look at the pictures and stories about three people. Describe the situations with the appropriate verbs and nouns. Then share your answers with your partner. (Answers may vary)

e.g.

What happened?

Alfred needed 300 bucks. Chad had 300 bucks.

➡ Chad lent Alfred 300 bucks.

A

What happened?

Joe got lost in the woods. Joan knows where to go.

➡ Joan _____ _____ the way.

B

What happened?

Ella was very thirsty. Ella ordered a bottle of water.

➡ A waiter _____ _____ _____ .

C

What happened?

Ashley wanted to have a nice dinner.
Austin is a good cook.

➡ Austin _____ _____ .

118 HighFive 1

06 Application

Exercise 7 Give your answers to the questions. Then practice with your partner. (Answers may vary)

e.g.
Q Who gave you a call yesterday?
A *My best friend gave me a call* .

A
Q Who bought you a drink last time?
A _____.

B
Q Who sent you a text message today?
A _____.

C
Q Who gave you a gift on your birthday?
A _____.

D
Q Who made you dinner yesterday?
A _____.

07 Discussion

Exercise 8 Read the following story and fill in the blanks with the given words. Share your ideas with your partner and present them to the whole class.

① emit   ② be capable of   ③ Charging   ④ autopilot   ⑤ distance

New electric big-rig revealed

Car company Eon has revealed a new big-rig truck. But, this is not just any truck. This truck is electric. Normally, only small cars were **A**_____ being electric. However, Eon has revealed that large big-rig trucks can be electric as well. Part of the reason for going electric is environmental. Many big-rig trucks have diesel engines. They **B**_____ large amounts of carbon dioxide into the air. Eon is hoping that their new electric car will have a positive impact on the environment. The new truck will need a very big battery to power it. Eon says that the battery in their trucks can go up to 500 miles on a single charge. However, that is about half the **C**_____ of what normal diesel trucks can do. **D**_____ the battery will take a couple of hours to accomplish, but for truck drivers' use on long trips, this won't be a problem. The new big-rigs will also be self-driving. The **E**_____ system will use cameras and sensors to help the car drive when in self-drive mode. Also, the size of the big-rig will be good for the massive super computer and cooling system needed to operate the self-driving function. Truck drivers, however, do not have to worry about losing their jobs to self-driving big-rigs. Human drivers will still be needed for picking up and dropping off their shipments.

Q1 Some people have voiced concerns that electric cars still pose risks. What do you think are the pros and cons of electric cars?

Q2 Why dose the battery in Eon's trucks, which only goes half the distance of a diesel engine, not pose a problem?

UNIT 15

I stopped drinking.

Unit Goals

Be able to talk about what you stopped doing.
Learn to use **"subject + verb + verb-ing"**

01 Brainstorming

Exercise 1 Look at the verbs in the two boxes (a) and (b), and find the difference between them.

(a)
I **learned** to swim.
I **plan** to leave tomorrow.
I **hope** to visit America.
I **expect** to hear good news.

(b)
I **stopped** drinking.
He **keeps** pushing me.
I **enjoy** watching movies.
I **finished** cleaning my room.

Exercise 2 Fill in the blanks with appropriate verbs above.

A I _enjoy_ staying alone at home.

B She never _____ talking.

C He _____ eating dinner before 6 p.m.

D You should _____ smoking.

E They _____ looking around in the mall.

F You should _____ working before midnight.

02 Grammar

Grammar Focus

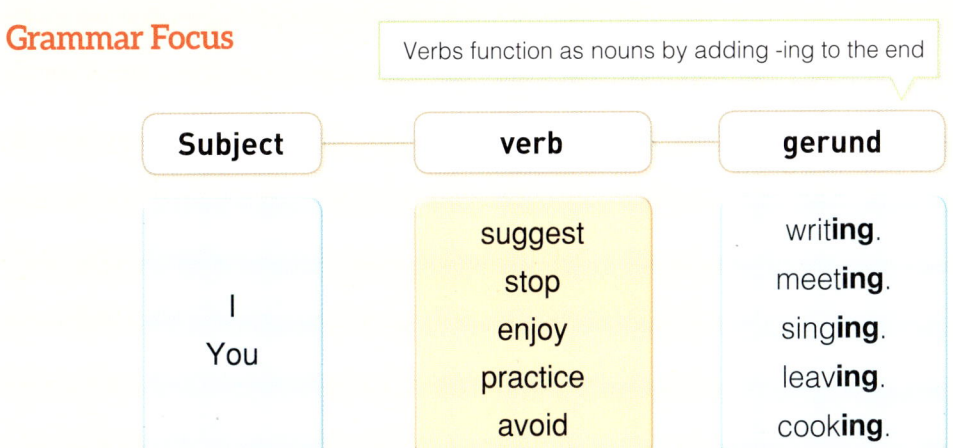

Exercise 3 Fill in the blanks with the appropriate forms of verbs from the boxes above.

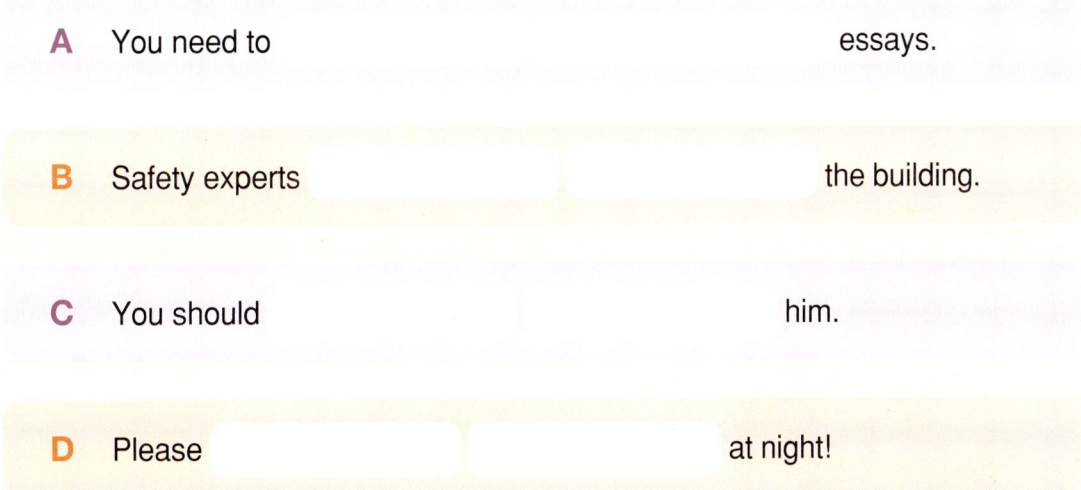

A You need to _____ essays.

B Safety experts _____ the building.

C You should _____ him.

D Please _____ at night!

Exercise 4 Look at the story in the box. Find the inappropriate forms of verbs and underline them. Then share your answer with your partner.

I was a high school English teacher. Last year, I _stopped to work_ and planned traveling around the world. I learned to drive a car and practiced to speak English. My parents kept worrying about me, but I really enjoyed to plan the trip!

03 Vocabulary

Exercise 5 Look at the pictures and conversations. Fill in the blanks with the appropriate words from each of the boxes. Then practice with your partner.

| a | quit   imagine   consider   give up   mind |

| b | live   jog   open   study   use |

e.g.
Dusty Let's go!
Christy No, I _quit jogging_ !!

A
Bryce I am tired of making travel plans.
Olivia You should consider _____ a travel agent next time.

B
Luke Do you mind _____ the window?
Rea No, not at all.

C
Shirley Stop using the cell phone!
Ned I can't _____ _____ without this.

D
Robin I got an F on the math exam.
Zack Don't _____ _____ math!

04 Dialogue

Exercise 6 Look at the conversation. Fill in the blanks with the appropriate words from the box below. Then listen to the conversation and practice with your partner.

> drink   play   say   keep   enjoy   learn   stop

Bellamy: Hey, do you want to have some beer after work?

Elliot: No, thanks. I _stopped drinking_.

Bellamy: What?! You're kidding. You _____ drinking every night.

Elliot: Not anymore!

Bellamy: Then what do you do after work?

Elliot: I enjoy _____ computer games. I am also considering _____ a new language.

Bellamy: Let's just have a glass of beer tonight!

Elliot: Stop _____ that! Go back to your seat and _____ working!

Bellamy: Ok… Let me know if you change your mind.

Unit15 I stopped drinking 125

05 Practice

Exercise 7 Look at the key words and sentences. Then change the sentences to the form of "verb + verb-ing" by using the key words. Practice with your partner by asking and answering questions about the sentences.

e.g.

Key word enjoy

I don't _like to ride_ **a bike.**
➡ I don't _enjoy riding_ a bike.

Q Do you enjoy riding a bike?
A No, I don't enjoy riding a bike.

A

Key word stop

I don't work for the company anymore.
➡ _____.

Q Did you stop _____?
A Yes, I _____.

B

Key word keep

I miss the last train every day.
➡ _____.

Q Do you keep _____?
A Yes, I _____.

06 Application

Exercise 8 Look at the three boxes of different verbs and use the phrases to practice with your partner. (Answers may vary)

Stop	Enjoy	Keep
1. exercise after work 2. drink 3. go to singing rooms	1. play computer games 2. talk on the phone 3. meet new people	1. work late 2. eat late at night 3. use public transportation to get to work

e.g.
Q Did you **stop exercising** after work?
A No, I didn't. I enjoy exercising after work.

Q
A

e.g.
Q Do you **enjoy meeting** new people?
A Yes, I do. I enjoy meeting new people.

Q
A

e.g.
Q Do you **keep working** late?
A Yes, I do. I keep working late these days.

Q
A

Unit15 I stopped drinking

07 Discussion

Exercise 9 Read the following story and fill in the blanks with the given words. Share your ideas with your partner and present them to the whole class.

① excitement ② switch ③ brainstorm ④ subscriptions ⑤ closets ⑥ rotate

Inside the offices of the business that lets you rent the latest fashions

A new company has a different approach to clothing: allowing customers to rent articles of clothing from over 450 fashion designers. Rent the Catwalk is a new company that offers monthly __A_____ for people to rent different fashion items. The offices of Rent the Catwalk are located in New York City, have 1,200  employees, but only have 250 people employed in their New York office. The lobby of the building has two __B_____ that __C_____ clothes inside them. This is part of the company's message that someone always has something to wear.

Each room of the building has a different look and feel. They have different purposes for workers that wants quiet spaces to work in or for someone who wants __D_____ when working with others on a project. Every piece of clothing that is offered on their website is photographed inside the office, and all clothing and accessories are kept in the office for future use. Desks in the office are in an open-floor style and employees __E_____ locations every six months. This allows employees to meet someone new and help __F_____ ideas.

Q1 What do you think of rented clothes? Would you rent clothes? What do you think would be the advantages and disadvantages of this business in Korea?

Q2 If you were conning a the clothes rental business, what kind of rental policies would you make? What should be considered in the business plan? What are customers likely to complain about?

UNIT 16

You decided to learn English!

Unit Goals

Be able to talk about what you decided to do.
Learn to use **"subject + verb + to-verb"**

01 Brainstorming

Exercise 1 Look at the sentences below. What is missing in the sentences?

> Today, I **wanted sleep** all day. But I **decided wake up** early because I **planned go** fishing. I left home early in the morning. Oops! I **forgot bring** my cell phone! I **need go** back home.

Exercise 2 Rewrite the sentences correctly.

A I _____ all day.

B But I _____ early because I _____ fishing.

C Oops! I _____ my cell phone!

D I _____ back home.

Exercise 3 Fill in the blanks with the appropriate words from the box above. (Answers may vary)

A I want _____ buy a nice car.

B I forgot _____ lock the door.

C I _____ take a day off.

D We _____ finish our work today.

E I _____ marry him.

02 Grammar

Grammar Focus

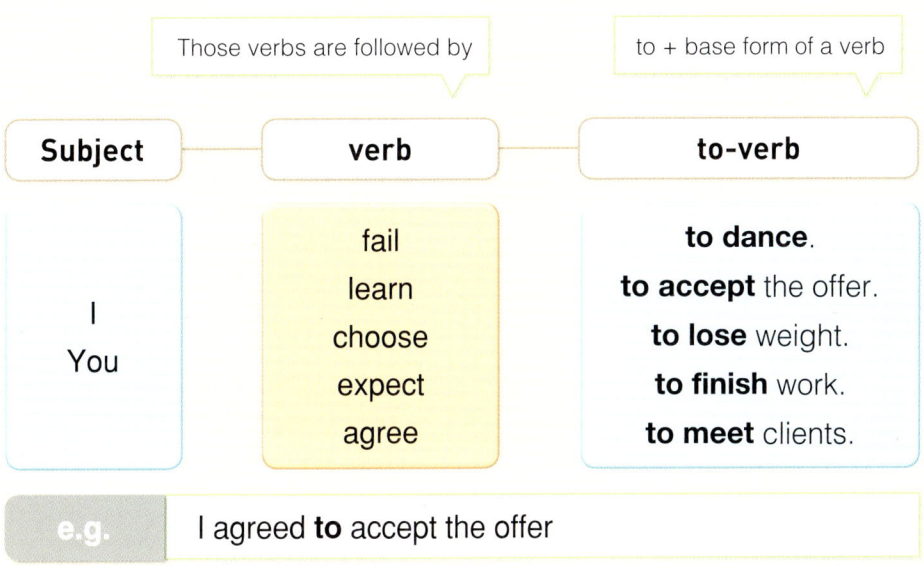

e.g. I agreed **to** accept the offer

Exercise 4 Fill in the blanks with appropriate words from the boxes above (#1-4). Then make two more sentences based on your own ideas (#5-6).

1. I chose _____ weight.

2. They _____ finish their work on time.

3. I expect _____ my clients.

4. She learned _____.

5. I failed _____.

6. I chose _____.

Unit16 You decided to learn English! 131

03 Vocabulary

Exercise 5 Look at the pictures and conversations. Fill in the blanks with the appropriate verbs from each of the boxes. Then practice with your partner.

| a | tend   refuse   afford   wish   promise |

| b | listen   overuse   live   deliver   buy |

e.g.
Emily How long does it take to deliver my bag?
Billy We _promise to deliver_ it within 3 days.

A
Jin Where do you want to live after retirement?
Blake I _____ live in Canada.

B
Ash What does she think about your advice?
Early She refused _____ to my advice.

C
Lisa Jim _____ his credit card.
Max You're right.

D
Brandon My parents want a big house.
Kirby Can they _____ a big house?

04 Dialogue

Exercise 6 Look at the conversation. Fill in the blanks with the appropriate words from the box below. Then listen to the conversation and practice with your partner.

> decide   learn   plan   need   want   fail

Marvin: Where did you go on your lunch break?

Lynn: I went to an English institute.

Marvin: Wow, you _decided to learn_ English!

Lynn: Not me. My husband _____ to study English, so I got a brochure for him.

Marvin: Why does he want to _____ it?

Lynn: Well, he had a meeting with American clients yesterday, but _____ to communicate with them.

Marvin: Oh…

Lynn: So, he feels like he _____ to study English.

Marvin: I see. When does he start?

Lynn: I don't know exactly, but he _____ to start from tomorrow.

Unit16 You decided to learn English! 133

05 Practice

Exercise 7 Look at the verbs and phrases. Use them to make 5 questions. Then practice with your partner by asking and answering the questions.

| want | need | decide | expect | plan |

| stay home | eat out | visit Paris | take a day off | win the contract |

e.g.
Q Do you *want to stay home* on the weekends?
A Yes, I do. I want to stay home on the weekends.
No, I don't. I don't want to stay home on the weekends.

A
Q Do you _____?
A _____.

B
Q Do you _____?
A _____.

C
Q Do you _____?
A _____.

D
Q Do you _____?
A _____.

06 Application

Exercise 8 Give your answers to the questions. Then practice with your partner. (Answers may vary)

Q Do you want to buy a new car?

e.g. A <u>Yes, I want to buy a new car</u> .

<u>No, I don't want to buy a new car</u> .

A
Q Do you want to sleep all day on the weekends?
A _____.

B
Q Do you plan to travel abroad on summer vacation?
A _____.

C
Q Do you tend to talk a lot?
A _____.

D
Q Do you wish to live in a different country after retirement?
A _____.

Unit16 You decided to learn English!

07 Discussion

Exercise 9 Read the following story and fill in the blanks with the given words. Share your ideas with your partner and present them to the whole class.

① obstacle ② comfort food ③ overcome ④ adapt ⑤ tough

Italian food having trouble in fast food arena

Hamburgers, pizza, and Mexican food have long dominated fast food dishes throughout America. However, Italian food is trying to make itself the next and best fast food dish. This is easier said than done. Part of the reason is that pasta is a __A__ food to __B__ to fast food standards. This is because it takes time to cook pasta and other Italian foods. Just boiling water to cook pasta noodles takes more time than grilling frozen meat patties. One way to __C__ this is a system of precooking, freezing, and flash-boiling noodles. This method has been shown to work, with pasta orders being completed in five minutes.

The next problem is a more difficult one. Pasta is, basically, a __D__. When people think of pasta, they think of sit-down restaurants or homemade dishes. People don't think of pasta as a fast food dish similar to hamburgers or pizza. Pasta is a food that should be eaten slowly, not quickly like other fast food dishes. This is the biggest __E__ in pasta's way towards becoming a fast food dish.

Q1 The size of the fast-food market is about 2 trillion won in Korea. Do you think it would be worthwhile to adapt Italian food to fast food dishes? What about traditional Korean dishes? What are the pros and cons of adapting traditional Korean food to fast food methods?

Q2 According the story, what are the main factors for food to be successful in the fast food industry?

UNIT 17

I want you to give a presentation.

Unit Goals

Be able to talk about what you want someone to do.
Learn to use **"subject + verb + noun + to-verb"**

01 Brainstorming

Exercise 1 Look at the verb phrases in the circle below and select the "things you want" and "things you want from your best friend."

Exercise 2 Fill in the blanks with your answers above. (Answers may vary)

A What do "you" want to do?

1. I want   *to meet new people*

2. I want

3. I want

B What do you want "your best friend" to do?

1. I want my best friend   *to meet new people*

2. I want my best friend

3. I want my best friend

02 Grammar

Grammar Focus

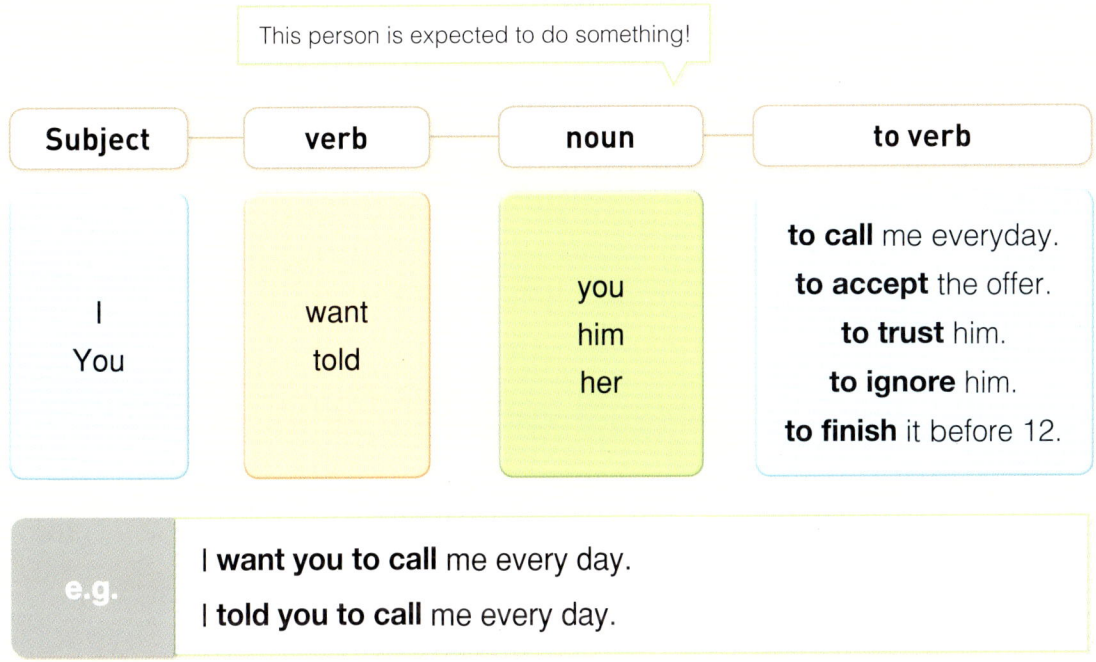

e.g.	I **want you to call** me every day.
	I **told you to call** me every day.

Exercise 3 Fill in the blanks with the words/phrases from the boxes above (#1-4). Then make two more sentences based on your ideas (#5-6). (Answers may vary.)

1. I _____ you to _____.

2. She told _____ to _____.

3. I _____ finish it before 12.

4. You told _____ to _____.

5. I want _____ to _____.

6. I told _____ to _____.

Unit17 I want you to give a presentation

03 Vocabulary

Exercise 4 Look at the pictures and conversations. Fill in the blanks with the appropriate verb phrases from the box. Then practice with your partner.

Verb phrases	clean up stop by the office google it meet at the airport send an email

e.g.
Chris   Hey, the boss _wants you to stop by his office_.
Billy   Hmm.. why?

A
Liz   I _____ you to _____ me _____ yesterday.
Hart   Oh, I'm sorry. I forgot.

B
Jasper   Son, I want _____ your room today.
Sam   Can I do it tomorrow?

C
Maggie   I told _____ me _____ at 7am.
Kelly   I'm sorry. I woke up late.

D
Jennifer   Hey, where can I get more information about the event?
Kay   I told _____.

140 HighFive 1

04 Dialogue

Exercise 6 Look at the conversation. Fill in the blanks with the appropriate words from the box below. Then listen to the conversation and practice with your partner.

| told   help   give a presentation   hurry   complete writing |

Kim: Mr. Wilson, where is the report?

Wilson: Um, what report do you mean?

Kim: I _____ you to _____ a sales report by noon today.

Wilson: Oops! I totally forgot…

Kim: What? I told you I want you *to give a presentation* about the report in a staff meeting!

Wilson: It will be on your desk by the end of the day, sir!

Kim: The meeting starts at 1pm today. You only have an hour, Mr.Wilson.

Wilson: Oh my…

Kim: Start writing it now! I want _____. I will tell Sarah _____ you.

Wilson: Yes, sir!

Unit17 I want you to give a presentation

05 Practice

Exercise 6 Look at the information and questions. Then make full sentences with on them. Share your answers with your partner.

e.g.

What happened?
- Claire is not happy.

Q What do you want?
A I want Claire to be happy.

A

What happened?
- Jack doesn't go to bed early.

Q What do you want?
A I want _____ early.

B

What happened?
- Mike sent me a fax today.

Q What did you tell him?
A I told _____ today.

C

What happened?
- Ruth doesn't finish her work on time.

Q What do you want?
A I _____ .

06 Application

Exercise 7 Give your answers to the questions. Then practice with your partner. (Answers may vary)

e.g.
Q What do you want your children to do?
A *I want my children to clean up their rooms* .

A
Q What do you want your colleague (or junior staffer) to do?
A _____.

B
Q What did you tell your colleague (or junior staffer) to do?
A _____.

C
Q What did your boss (or team leader) want you to do?
A _____.

D
Q What did your boss (or team leader) tell you to do?
A _____.

07 Discussion

Exercise 9 Read the following story and fill in the blanks with the given words. Share your ideas with your partner and present them to the whole class.

① without ② depressed ③ sense ④ overwhelmed ⑤ full-time ⑥ part time

More young Americans out of high school are also out of work

The recent news that college graduates work as baristas or clerks makes us __A_____. The John J. Heldrich Center for Workforce Development at Rutgers University reported an even gloomier story. When it comes to less-educated people the situation is far worse. For this group, finding work that pays a living wage and gives __B_____ of security is very hard to find. Walter Walden, 24, said, "I want more money, and I really don't like what I do. I had to go back to school." He now lives with his mother so he can take nursing classes __C_____.

The economy is temporarily weak and traditional middle class jobs are dwindling over the longer term. These workers are __D_____ by that. Americans who graduated from high school were having trouble making ends meet. Just 37 percent employed were full-time. Another 23 percent were working part time, usually because they could not find __E_____ work. The national conversation is about whether college is worth it, despite the debt and burden that higher education causes. However, most high school graduates without college still believe they would be unable to get good jobs __F_____ more education.

Q1 Who do you know who has chosen a career out of high school instead of going on to college?

Q2 What do you think their decision?

18 UNIT

It made me cough.

Unit Goals

Be able to talk about what someone makes you do.
Learn to use **"subject + causative verb + noun + verb or adjective"**

01 Brainstorming

Exercise 1 Look at the pictures and sentences. Then find answers to the questions based on the given information.

Carol made Austin lie.

1. Who lied? _Austin_
2. Who made him do it? _Carol_

Derek let me join the club.

1. Who joined the club? _____
2. Who let you do it? _____

Young let James leave early.

1. Who left early? _____
2. Who let him do it? _____

Drinking wine makes Kristal smile

1. Who smiles? _____
2. What makes her do it? _____

Pollen makes Jenny cough.

1. Who coughs? _____
2. What makes her do it? _____

02 Grammar

Grammar Focus

"Subject" caused "noun" to "do something"

Subject	causative verb	noun	verb
I You It	let have make	me you him her	**call** you. **know** the secret. **feel** better. **work** hard. **use** the computer.

e.g.
He **let me use** his computer.
He **made me happy**.

Tip! Adjectives can also be used after "make"

Exercise 2 Fill in the blanks with words/phrases from the boxes above (#1-4). Then make a sentence based on your own idea (#5) (Answers may vary.)

1. He made _____ _____ hard.

2. Running makes _____ _____.

3. You let me _____.

4. I'll have my assistant _____.

5. _____.

Unit18 It made me cough

03 Vocabulary

Exercise 3 Look at the pictures and conversations. Fill in the blanks with appropriate causative verbs and/ or verb phrases from the box. Then practice with your partner.

Verb & phrases	make let say it again feel good happen again dry overnight wear the hat

e.g.

Harper Do you like this song?

Emma Yes, it _makes_ me feel _good_.

A

Logan Hey, look at me! Noah _____ me _____.

Benjamin It looks good on you!

B

Mia Clean up this room. Don't _____ me _____.

Sam Yes, mom.

C

Isabella This t-shirt is still dripping wet.

Sophia _____ it _____.

D

Olivia I am sorry I missed the meeting today.

William Don't _____ it _____!

148 HighFive 1

04 Dialogue

Exercise 6 Look at the conversation. Fill in the blanks with the appropriate words from the box below. Then listen to the conversation and practice with your partner.

> make   let   feel better   nervous   cough
> bother you   go home early

Jane: Hey Eden, how was your job interview last week?

Eden: It wasn't good.

Jane: What happened?

Eden: I had the flu that day. It _made_ me _cough_ throughout the interview.

Jane: Hmm…

Eden: So, the interviewer _____ me _____.

Jane: Oh, man… did you get the job?

Eden: I don't know. It _____ me so _____. I can't sleep at night.

Jane: Don't let it _____.

Eden: Yeah, I try not to think about it.

Jane: Good. Let's go jogging. It will _____ you _____.

Unit 18 It made me cough   149

05 Practice

Exercise 5 Look at the conversations and complete the conversations with the causative verbs given in the boxes. Then practice with your partner. (Answers may vary)

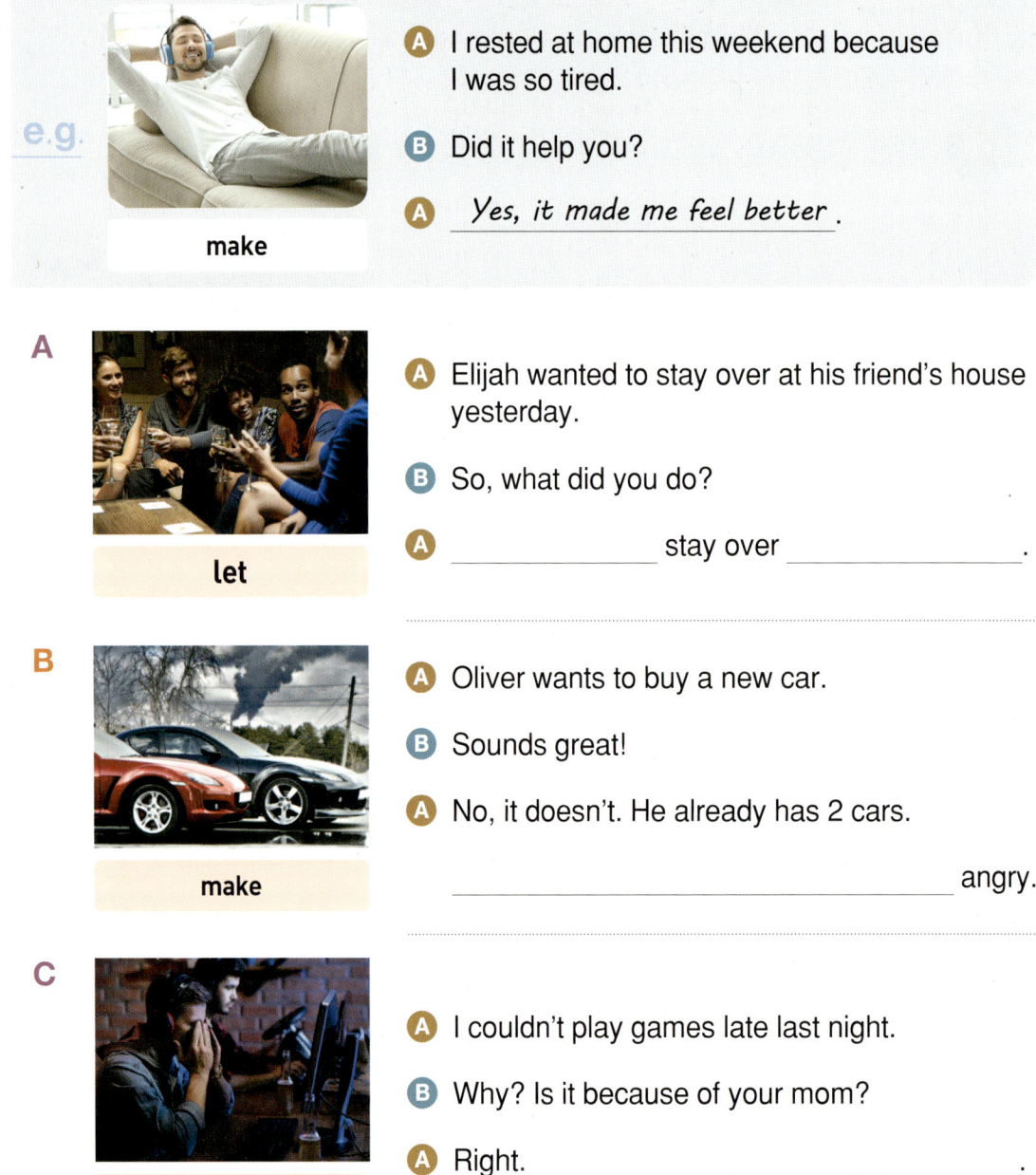

e.g.

Ⓐ I rested at home this weekend because I was so tired.
Ⓑ Did it help you?
Ⓐ <u>Yes, it made me feel better</u>.

make

A
Ⓐ Elijah wanted to stay over at his friend's house yesterday.
Ⓑ So, what did you do?
Ⓐ _____ stay over _____.

let

B
Ⓐ Oliver wants to buy a new car.
Ⓑ Sounds great!
Ⓐ No, it doesn't. He already has 2 cars.
_____ angry.

make

C
Ⓐ I couldn't play games late last night.
Ⓑ Why? Is it because of your mom?
Ⓐ Right. _____.

let

06 Application

Exercise 6 Look at the two boxes of causative verbs. Make 2 questions by using the verb phrases. Then practice with your partner.

let
1. drive your car
2. use your computer
3. stay at your house

e.g.
Q Do you let your friend drive your car?
A Yes, I do. (I let my friend drive my car)
         or
   No, I don't. (I don't let my friend drive my car)

make
1. sing songs
2. talk in English
3. travel alone

e.g.
Q How does singing songs make you feel?
A It makes me feel good.

A
Q Do you _____ ?
A _____.

B
Q How does _____ ?
A _____.

Unit18 It made me cough

07 Discussion

Exercise 7 Read the following story and fill in the blanks with the given words. Share your ideas with your partner and present them to the whole class.

① splashing ② soaring ③ reach ④ by ⑤ runs ⑥ tourists

Correspondents, 10 Drives, California's Route

The Pacific Coast Highway **A**_____ along much of the California coast. It is probably one of the most iconic roads in the country, has appeared in film and has been visited by **B**_____.

My favorite stretch is in Malibu. That road has a sunny blur of California coast: beaches, mountains, ocean, wetlands, and surfers. When you start from Santa Monica on Route 1 heading north, the highway's charms are hidden at first. You will pass the row of millionaire's homes which are unbelievably modest and hidden **C**_____ shrubs.

From there, the coastline appears around every turn and over every hill. You will see the sparkling surf on your left, green hills and red cliffs on your right. At Point Dume State Beach, there are **D**_____ cliffs and dolphins and sea lions **E**_____ in the water.

At El Matador Beach, up the road, there is a hidden world that has interesting rock formations, pools, and sandy coves. Remember though, that you have to walk down a lot of steps to **F**_____ it. If you want a dramatic return, take Route 23 through the Santa Monica Mountains back to Los Angeles. The road is an ear-popping, heart-stopping 14 miles or so. After this drive you will never think of Los Angeles the same way again.

Q1 Tell us about road trips you've taken or dreamed about.

Q2 Around your neighborhood, what journeys would you recommend to people who don't know the area?

UNIT 19

Every time I try to play tennis, it rains.

Unit Goals

Be able to combine two sentences.
Learn to use **"conjunction + subject + verb, subject + verb"**

01 Brainstorming

Exercise 1 Look at the two boxes below. Find sentences that are related to each other. Then draw a line between the two sentences.

- I woke up in the morning.
- We're together.
- I want to meet you.
- I wash my car.
- You can stay with me.

- It rains the next day.
- You are busy.
- I felt refreshed.
- You would like.
- We can do anything.

Exercise 2 Fill in the blanks based on Paul's story. Then practice with your partner.

A **When** I woke up in the morning, *I felt refreshed* .

B **Every time** I wash my car, _____ .

C **As long as** we're together, _____ .

D **Every time** I want to meet you, _____ .

E You can stay with me **as long as** _____ .

02 Grammar

Grammar Focus

This is used to connect clauses or sentences!

conjunction	subject+verb	(comma)	subject+verb
When Every time As long as	I am alive I was a child I call you	,	I lived by the sea. a different person answers. that's impossible.

Exercise 3 Make full sentences from the sentences and conjunctions above.

A When _____, I lived by the sea.

B _____ I am alive, _____.

C _____ I call you, _____.

Exercise 4 Find appropriate answers to the following questions from Exercise 3 and practice with your partner by asking and answering the questions.

A Can you give me a call?

B Please sir, may I marry your daughter?

C When did you live by the sea?

03 Vocabulary

Exercise 5 Look at the pictures and conversations. Fill in the blanks with the appropriate conjunctions and/ or clauses from the boxes. Then practice with your partner.

conjunction	Clause 1	Clause 2
when every time as long as	The price is reasonable I sleep at night He looks at me You pay a fee	My heart skips a beat You can join I leave the lights on We should renew the contract

A

Judy How can I become a member of this club?

Denis As long as _____, you can join.

B

Mona _____ he looks at me, _____.

Maia Oh, you fell for him!

C

Hoyt Are you scared of the dark?

Lea Yes, _____ I sleep at night, _____.

D

Olivia What do you think about this contract?

Sarah _____, we should renew the contract.

156 HighFive 1

04 Dialogue

Exercise 6 Look at the conversation. Fill in the blanks with the appropriate words from the box below. Then listen to the conversation and practice with your partner.

> it rains   every time   as long as   call me   when

Harper: Not again!

Emily: Hey, you look annoyed. What's up?

Harper: _Every time_ I try to play tennis, _____!

Emily: Why don't you look for an indoor tennis court?

Harper: I can't find one in my neighborhood.

Emily: _____ you don't mind traveling a little bit, I can recommend one near my house.

Harper: Thanks! I used to play tennis there. But afterwards I felt tired _____ returning home.

Emily: If you want to come again, _____. We can play together.

Unit19 Every time I try to play tennis, it rains   157

05 Practice

Exercise 7 Look at the pictures and key words. Then complete the conversations by using the key words and appropriate conjunctions and practice with your partner. (Answers may vary)

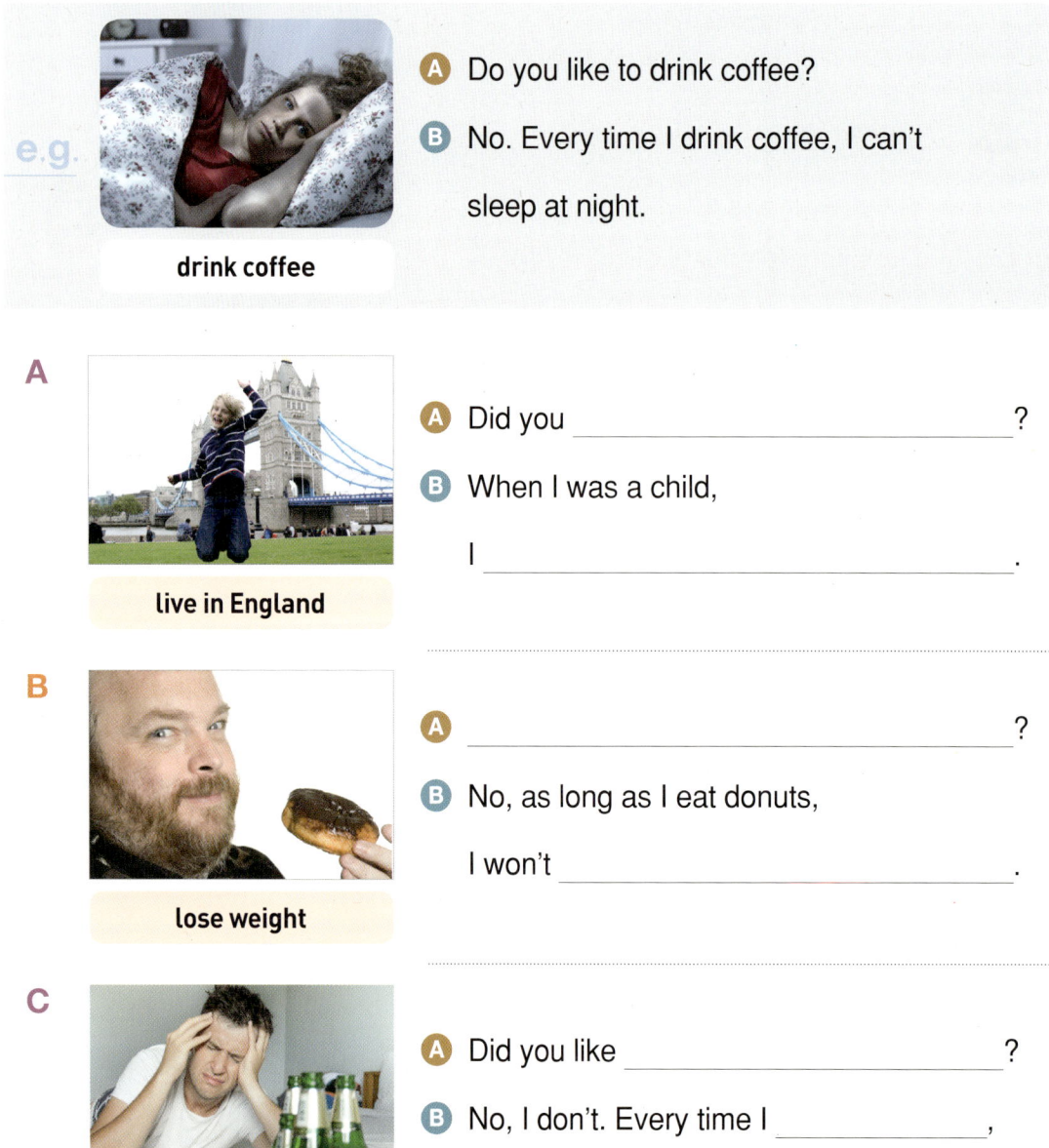

e.g.
- **A** Do you like to drink coffee?
- **B** No. Every time I drink coffee, I can't sleep at night.

drink coffee

A
- **A** Did you _____?
- **B** When I was a child, I _____.

live in England

B
- **A** _____?
- **B** No, as long as I eat donuts, I won't _____.

lose weight

C
- **A** Did you like _____?
- **B** No, I don't. Every time I _____, I have a bad headache.

like drinking beer

06 Application

Exercise 8 Ask your partner two questions and your partner should answer the questions by using "when," "every time," or "as long as."

Q   Do you like playing soccer?
e.g. A   Yes. When I was a kid, I liked playing soccer.
    Every time I play soccer, I am happy.

A
Q _____?
A _____.

B
Q _____?
A _____.

Unit19 Every time I try to play tennis, it rains

07 Discussion

Exercise 9 Read the following story and fill in the blanks with the given words. Share your ideas with your partner and present them to the whole class.

① firmly   ② like   ③ as   ④ curved   ⑤ comes   ⑥ leave

Rediscovering a shortcut to an hourglass figure

Fajas __A_____ in a variety of shapes and sizes, from full-body jumpsuits to tight belly bands, for women as well __B_____ men. The effects depend on what kind of fabric the fajas are made of. They come in Lycra, cotton, nylon and latex. The tighter the material, the more flattering the effect. Prices range from $20 to over $70. It depends on the fabric and how much of the body it covers. Lilliana Rios, 33 writes about the faja on her blog, "There is a Spanish saying, you want to look __C_____ a Coke bottle. A lot of Spanish songs talk about women with shapes like a guitar, so that's the __D_____ look that Latina women want."

When a woman puts on a faja, it will be uncomfortable. It must be closed __E_____ against the skin by hooks and a zipper and a can force the air out of your lungs. It sounds sexy, but fajas are not. Most are the color of an Ace bandage and look like body casts. Some squeeze certain areas and __F_____ others loose.

Q1 Tell us about the compromises you've made to fashion, style, or beauty, at any point in your life.

Q2 Do you think it's worth being uncomfortable to look good?

UNIT 20

I heard it's Edward.

Unit Goals

Be able to talk about what you heard and thought.
Learn to use **"subject + verb + (that) + subject + verb"**

01 Brainstorming

Exercise 1 Look at the sentences in the box and divide them into the two boxes on the right "heard" and "thought". (e.g., if you think the sentence is something a person heard from someone, put the word in the "heard" box) Answers may vary.

The movie is coming out soon.
We were friends.
You had a car accident.
You needed more sleep.
You were 30, at most.
You had a baby girl.

heard

thought

Exercise 2 Fill in the blanks based on your answers above. Then practice with your partner.

A I *heard* that *the movie is coming out soon* .

B I thought that _____ .

C I heard that _____ .

D I _____ that _____ .

E I _____ that _____ .

F I _____ that _____ .

162 HighFive 1

02 Grammar

Grammar Focus

This is used to connect the two sentences!

subject + verb	conjunction	subject + verb
I heard I thought	(that)	you're looking for a house. you were angry about something. he's rich. you left the company. the price was ridiculous.

Exercise 3 Make appropriate sentences with the expressions above. Then practice the conversations with your partner.

A
- A: _____ ?
- B: Yes, he is a millionaire.

B
- A: _____ ?
- B: You're right. It was too expensive.

C
- A: _____ ?
- B: No, I wasn't.

D
- A: _____ ?
- B: Yeah, I quit the job.

E
- A: _____ ?
- B: Yes, my family is planning to move next month.

Unit20 I heard it's Edward

03 Vocabulary

Exercise 4 Look at the pictures and conversations. Fill in the blanks with the appropriate causative verbs and or verb phrases from the boxes. Then practice with your partner.

Verb	Verb phrases
heard thought	break up work for Google open a new restaurant be my best friend be the ideal couple know each other talk about me behind my back

A

Lynn   I _heard_ you _work for Google_.

Sage   Yes, that's right.

Lynn   Oh. I _____ you wanted to _____.

B

Taylor   Look who's there. It's Jamie!

Scott   Who's he?

Taylor   Oh, I _____ you _____.

C

Andrew   Are Henry and Amy coming for dinner tonight?

Lucas   I don't think so. I _____ they _____.

Andrew   Really? I _____ they _____.

D

Marie   Hey, I heard you are _____.

Lila   Uh, well…

Marie   I _____ you _____.

164 HighFive 1

04 Dialogue

Exercise 6 Look at the conversation. Fill in the blanks with the appropriate words from the box below. Then listen to the conversation and practice with your partner.

> heard   thought   get promoted   be qualified
> renew a contract   an easy-going person

Jeremy: Do you know who our new manager is?

Abigail: _I heard_ it's Edward.

Jeremy: Really? I _____ it would be Vanessa.

Abigail: I _____ she didn't _____ this time.

Jeremy: Oh, why? I _____ she _____ for the position.

Abigail: I agree, but I _____ she failed to _____ with the supplier.

Jeremy: Hmm, what do you think about Edward?

Abigail: Well, I don't know him very well, but I _____ that he is pretty strict.

Jeremy: Oh, I _____ he _____.

05 Practice

Exercise 6 Pair work – Look at the pictures and questions. Then complete the conversations by using the verbs "heard" or "thought" with and clauses. Then practice with your partner. (Answers may vary)

e.g.

Blake   tough   nurse

Q Is Blake a doctor?
A _I heard he is a nurse_ .

Q He's very tough, right?
A _Oh, I thought he was sensitive_ .

A

Nick and Daisy   a child

Q Do Nick and Daisy have three children?
A _____ .

Q Did you know they have a daughter?
A _____ .

B

Mac   Korean American who was born in Korea

Q Is Mac a Korean?
A _____ .

Q Did you know he was born in Korea?
A _____ .

 Application

Exercise 7 Ask your partner two questions and your partner should answer the questions by using "heard" or "thought."

e.g.
Q Have you heard of Leonardo DiCaprio?
A Yes, I heard his new movie is really good .

A
Q _____?
A _____.

e.g.
Q Did you know he's American ?
A Oh, I thought he was an Australian.

B
Q _____?
A _____.

07 Discussion

Exercise 8 Read the following story and fill in the blanks with the given words. Share your ideas with your partner and present them to the whole class.

① gulp ② bubble ③ piece ④ tone ⑤ sacrificed ⑥ touch

When Did You Last Have a Great Conversation?

The psychologist Sherry Turkle says that "we have __A__ conversation" because of habits like texting and using social media. We are together, but each of us is in our own __B__, furiously connected to keyboards and tiny touch screens.

In the silence of connection, people are comforted when they are in __C__ with a lot of people. We can't get enough of one another, if we can use technology to keep one another at distances that we can control: not too close, not too far, but just right. Texting, e-mail, and posting let us present the self we want to be. If we wish to, we can delete or alter the voice, the flesh, the face, and the body. Not too much, not too little — just right.

We easily think that our little "sips" of online connection become a big __D__ of real conversation. But they don't. But no matter how valuable, they do not substitute for conversation. Connecting in sips may work for gathering a __E__ of information. But connecting in sips doesn't work as well when it comes to understanding and knowing one another. In conversation we care for one another. We can pay attention to __F__ and nuance. In conversation, we are called upon to see things from another's point of view.

Q1 When do you prefer a conversation to an exchange of texts?

Q2 When did you recently have a great conversation with someone?

Answer Key

UNIT 01
She is an American actress.

03 Vocabulary
Exercise 4
homemaker   actor   lawyer   celebrity   office worker   journalist

Exercise 5
A) celebrity
B) is a homemaker
C) He was, is a journalist
D) He is an office worker
E) are lawyers

04 Dialogue
Exercise 6
She is, is she, is her, she is
she is not, old is she, She is, That's

05 Practice
Exercise 7
A) Q What's her name?   A Her name is Jessica Miller.
   Q How old is she?   A She is 22 years old.
   Q What is her job?   A She is a cheerleader.

B) Q What's his name?   A His name is Andrew Horton.
   Q How old is he?   A He is 53 years old.
   Q What is his job?   A He is a priest.

C) Q What's her name?   A Her name is Dana Rodgers.
   Q How old is she?   A She is 31 years old.
   Q What is her job   A She is a fashion designer.

Exercise 8
What's his name? His name is Harry Linden,
What is his job? He is a chief manager.
What is his phone number? His office number is 202-450-3915, and the mobile number is 614-948-2531.
What is his email address? His email address is Linden.harry@oia.org.

07 Discussion
Exercise 10
A ③   B ①   C ④   D ②   E ⑤

UNIT 02
He's an easygoing guy.

03 Vocabulary
Exercise 4
b-8, c-6, d-1, e-2, f-3, g-10, h-5, i-7, j-9

Exercise 5
(answers may vary)
A) a strict teacher.
B) My parents are amazing people.
C) My husband is a lucky man.

04 Dialogue
Exercise 6
He is, Is he, well-known, helpful, introverted, brave

05 Practice
Exercise 7
A) His name is Brad Carter. He is 37 years old. He drinks beer a lot. He is a heavy drinker.
B) Her name is Ellen Baker. She is 4 years old. She doesn't like vegetables. She is a picky eater.
C) Her name is Jenny Cox. She is 9 years old. She learns new things fast. She is a fast learner.

Exercise 8
(Answers may vary)
Her name is Dana Spencer. She is 23 years old. She is an outgoing person. She likes to go to parties and dance. She is a good dancer.

07 Discussion
Exercise 10
A ④   B ③   C ①   D ②   E ⑤

UNIT 03
There is a bag on the bench.

03 Vocabulary
Exercise 4
A) Are there / under
   are three girls under the tree
B) in front of the house
   a guy in front of the house
C) Is there / behind
   is a boy behind
D) on
   a guy on the sofa
E) there a dog next to
   next to

04 Dialogue
Exercise 5
was there, Is there, in, in, there a cell phone in the bag,

isn't, there was, on, There is

05 Practice
Exercise 6
A) There is
B) Are there
C) Are, there are
D) Is there, there isn't, is a cup
E) Are there, there are

07 Discussion
Exercise 8
A ⑤   B ①   C ③   D ②   E ④

UNIT 04
You were very excited about the trip!

03 Vocabulary
Exercise 4
A) calm   B) disappointed   C) confused   D) confident
E) embarrassed

04 Dialogue
Exercise 5
embarrassed, happy, was, annoyed

05 Practice
Exercise 6
(answers may vary)
A) was so nervous   B) was relieved
C) was embarrassed   D) was happy
E) was very tired

07 Discussion
Exercise 8
A ②   B ④   C ⑥   D ③   E ①   F ⑤

UNIT 05
I am tired of them.

03 Vocabulary
Exercise 4
A) happy with   B) worried about   C) disappointed in
D) sure of

Exercise 5
A) Are, disappointed in   B) Are you sure of
C) Is, worried about

04 Dialogue
Exercise 6
disappointed in, surprised at, jealous of, worried about, scared of

05 Practice
Exercise 7
(answers may vary)
A) A Chris plays computer games every day.
   B Is he crazy about them?
   A Yes, he is crazy about computer games.
B) A Helen and James are moving to a new city next week
   B Are they worried about it?
   A Yes, they are worried about moving.
C) A Kate has a blind date tomorrow.
   B Is she excited about it?
   A No, she is very nervous about the date.

07 Discussion
Exercise 10
A ①   B ②   C ③   D ④   E ⑤   F ⑥

UNIT 06
It is hard to wake up early in the morning.

03 Vocabulary
Exercise 4
(answers may vary)
A) easy, hear your voice
B) great, see you again
C) difficult, speak in person
D) important, remember people's names
E) better, take a taxi

Exercise 5
A) Is, difficult to   B) it easy   C) Is it better

04 Dialogue
Exercise 6
is better to, easy to, interesting to, difficult to, is important to

05 Practice
Exercise 7
(answers may vary)
A) A Is it nice to go to Europe in summer?
   B Yes, it is so nice (to go to Europe in summer).

Answer Key **171**

B) **A** Is it difficult to drive a car in rush hour?
   B Yes, it is so difficult (to drive a car in rush hour).
C) **A** Is it scary to watch horror movies at night?
   B No, it's not scary (to watch horror movies at night).
D) **A** Is it better to eat breakfast in the morning?
   B Yes, it is better (to eat breakfast in the morning).

07 Discussion
Exercise 10
A ④ B ② C ① D ③ E ⑤

UNIT 07
I got worried about you.

03 Vocabulary
Exercise 4
A) married, got married   B) hurt, got hurt
C) divorced, got divorced   D) worried, got worried
E) thirsty, get thirsty

04 Dialogue
Exercise 5
get hurt, got tired, get mad, nervous

05 Practice
Exercise 6
(Answers may vary)
A) **A** Robin worked overtime every night
   B Oh, did he get tired of working?
   A Yes, he got tired of working.
B) **A** Terry fell off her bicycle.
   B Oh, did she get hurt?
   A No, she didn't get hurt.
C) **A** Luke's GPS didn't work this morning.
   B Oh, did he get lost?
   A Yes, he got lost.

07 Discussion
Exercise 10
A ⑤ B ② C ① D ③ E ④

UNIT 08
It smells great!

03 Vocabulary
Exercise 4
A) sour   B) sorry
C) ridiculous   D) terrible

E) comfortable

04 Dialogue
Exercise 5
great, Sounds, delicous, looks, tastes

05 Practice
Exercise 6
(answers may vary)
A) Ivan feels bad / Ivan feels disappointed /
   I feel sorry for him
B) It sounds interesting / Valerie feels excited /
   Valerie looks happy
C) Adrian feels terrible / It sounds serious /
   Adrian feels disappointed in him

07 Discussion
Exercise 10
A ⑤ B ③ C ① D ⑥ E ② F ④

UNIT 09
It looks like a snake.

03 Vocabulary
Exercise 4

historical — concerned with events of the past
endless — to have no end
lengthy — too long
temporary — lasting for a time only
up to date — latest
tremendous — vast, huge

04 Dialogue
Exercise 6
has been, since, been, been, should, be, It's

05 Practice
Exercise 8
(answers may vary)
A) It has been a month since I called Mom.
B) It's been a year since I worked at my previous office.
C) It's been 6 months since I practiced speaking Chinese.

07 Discussion
Exercise 10
A ④ B ⑥ C ① D ② E ③ F ⑤

UNIT 10
He talks too much.

03 Vocabulary
Exercise 4
(answers may vary)
A) sob / sobs a lot
B) stretch / stretch a lot
C) dance / dances all the time
D) smile / smile all the time

04 Dialogue
Exercise 5
complains, drinks, sleep

05 Practice
Exercise 6
A) Claire feels tired because her husband snores all night.
B) Daisy felt annoyed because the dog next door barked all night.

07 Discussion
Exercise 10
A ④   B ③   C ①   D ⑥   E ②   F ⑤

UNIT 11
I couldn't sleep last night.

03 Vocabulary
Exercise 4
A) last, lasts
B) depart, departs
C) come, came
D) exist, exist

04 Dialogue
Exercise 5
studied, barked, arrived, sitting

05 Practice
Exercise 6
(answers may vary)
A) responds to my email
B) are running to the station
C) ate before class

07 Discussion
Exercise 10
A ⑤   B ①   C ④   D ②   E ③

UNIT 12
I didn't attend the meeting.

03 Vocabulary
Exercise 4
A) meet
B) contact
C) discuss
D) lacks
E) resembles

04 Dialogue
Exercise 5
contact, answer, meet, discuss

05 Practice
Exercise 6
A) A receive Mr. Tyler's email
   B received it
B) A contact the client
   B contacted him (or her)
C) A enter the university
   B entered it
D) A walk your dog
   B walk him (or her)

07 Discussion
Exercise 10
A ①   B ④   C ③   D ⑤   E ②

UNIT 13
I ask him for an autograph.

03 Vocabulary
Exercise 4
A) asked
B) Thank, the ride
C) dress, paid
D) Thank, your help
E) asked, coffee

04 Dialogue
Exercise 5
coming, paid, the ticket, service fees

05 Practice
Exercise 6
A) asked you for fried chicken
B) paid a lot of money for it
C) Thank you for inviting me.

07 Discussion
Exercise 10
A ④ B ③ C ⑤ D ② E ①

UNIT 14
Did you send me a text?

03 Vocabulary
Exercise 4
A) bought, a secondhand car
B) lend me, money
C) read, this letter
D) made me

04 Dialogue
Exercise 5
gave, ask, questions, a presentation, teach, how to prepare

05 Practice
Exercise 6
A) told Joe
B) gave Ella a bottle of water
C) made her a nice dinner

07 Discussion
Exercise 10
A ② B ① C ⑤ D ③ E ④

UNIT 15
I stopped drinking.

03 Vocabulary
Exercise 5
A) using
B) opening
C) imagine living
D) give up studying

04 Dialogue
Exercise 6
enjoyed, playing, learning, saying, keep

05 Practice
Exercise 7
A) I stopped working for the company.
 Q working for the company?
 A Yes, I stopped working for the company.

B) I keep missing the last train.
 Q missing the last train
 A keep missing the last train

07 Discussion
Exercise 10
A ④ B ⑤ C ⑥ D ① E ② F ③

UNIT 16
You decided to learn English!

03 Vocabulary
Exercise 5
A) wish to
B) to listen
C) tends to overuse
D) afford to buy

04 Dialogue
Exercise 6
wants, learn, failed, needs, plans

05 Practice
Exercise 7
(answers may vary)
A) Do you need to take a day off?
 Yes, I do. I need to take a day off.
B) Do you want to stay home?
 No, I don't. I don't want to stay home.
C) Do you expect to win the contract?
 Yes, I do. I expect to win the contract.
D) Do you plan to visit Paris?
 Yes, I do. I plan to visit Paris.
E) Do you want to eat out tonight?
 No, I don't. I don't want to eat out tonight.

07 Discussion
Exercise 10
A ⑤ B ④ C ③ D ② E ①

UNIT 17
I want you to give a presentation.

03 Vocabulary
Exercise 4
A) told, send, an email
B) you to clean up
C) you to meet, at the airport

D) you to google it

04 Dialogue
Exercise 5
told, complete writing, you to hurry, to help

05 Practice
Exercise 6
A) Jack to go to bed
B) Mike to send me a fax
C) want Ruth to finish her work on time

07 Discussion
Exercise 10
A ②   B ③   C ⑥   D ④   E ⑤   F ①

UNIT 18
It made me cough.

03 Vocabulary
Exercise 3
A) made, wear the (this) hat   B) make, say it again
C) Let, dry overnight   D) let, happen again

04 Dialogue
Exercise 4
made, go home early, makes, nervous, bother you, make, feel better

05 Practice
Exercise 5
(answers may vary)
A) I let him, at his friend's house.
B) He makes me feel
C) She didn't let me do it.
   (She didn't let me play games late)

07 Discussion
Exercise 10
A ⑤   B ⑥   C ④   D ②   E ①   F ③

UNIT 19
Every time I try to play tennis, it rains.

03 Vocabulary
Exercise 5
A) you pay a fee
B) Every time, my heart skips a beat
C) when, I leave the lights on
D) As long as the price is reasonable

04 Dialogue
Exercise 6
it rains, As long as, when, call me

05 Practice
Exercise 7
(answers may vary)
A) A Did you live in England?
   B I was a kid / I lived in England
B) A Did you lose some weight?
   B I eat donuts / I won't lose weight
C) A Do you like drinking beer?
   B No. Every time I drink beer / I get a bad headache

07 Discussion
Exercise 10
A ⑤   B ③   C ②   D ④   E ①   F ⑥

UNIT 20
I heard it's Edward.

03 Vocabulary
Exercise 4
A) thought, open a new restaurant
B) thought, know each other
C) heard, broke up, thought, were the ideal couple
D) talking about me behind my back, thought, are my best friend

04 Dialogue
Exercise 5
thought, heard, get promoted, thought, was qualified, heard, renew a contract, heard, thought, is an easy-going person

05 Practice
Exercise 6
A) I heard they have one child.
   Oh, I thought they have a boy.
B) I heard he is Korean-American
   Oh, I thought he was born in America

07 Discussion
Exercise 10
A ⑤   B ②   C ⑥   D ①   E ③   F ④

www.hicalling.co.kr

어렵다! 막막하다! 포기말고

Hi Calling

믿고 맡기는 강사진. 국내 대기업에서 직원 외국어 교육으로 수년간 검증받은 우수 HiEnglish 강사진 그대로 전화 외국어 강의합니다.

수준별 체계적 교재. 17년간 기업 교육 전문 HiEnglish가 만든 수준별 교재와 동영상 강의로 오랫동안 재미있게 학습하며 실력을 향상합니다.

고객 감동. 고객을 먼저 생각하는 외국어 교육으로 정성을 다하겠습니다.

하이콜링 신청하기

| 고객센터 전화 상담신청 02)6677-2770 | HiSume앱 상담신청 버튼 (이름/연락처) | 온라인 레벨테스트 | 기업 출강 경력 원어민 강사 매칭 |

하이콜링 할인 혜택
10% DOWN
Hight Five ❶ 교재를 구입하신 분에게는 하이콜링 **10% 할인제공!**

 하이콜링 상담 전화 02-6677-2770
서울시 마포구 서교동 355-32 하이잉글리쉬 T. 02-335-1002 F. 02-335-0121
E. hicalling2@hienglish.com

 Play 스토어에서 [하주메] 검색